Petra Thiemann ● David F

Creating

user-friendly

Online Help

Basics and Implementation

with MadCap Flare

This book was first published in German by Vieweg+Teubner in 2008.

The title of the original book is "Benutzerfreundliche Online-Hilfen: Grundlagen und Umsetzung mit MadCap Flare" by Petra Thiemann. ISBN of original book is 978-3834804242

Publishing rights for English edition are courtesy of Petra Thiemann.

Published by David Krings through CreateSpace, 2009.

ISBN for this book: 978-1449952037

This book was created with OpenOffice.org 3.1 and MadCap Capture.

Foreword

Some would question the need for a new authoring tool in the documentation industry such as MadCap Flare. To answer this question we need to look back at the beginnings of the industry.

In the early days of Microsoft Windows, Microsoft developed a new documentation format for PC-based documentation called WinHelp. The WinHelp format was a major breakthrough bringing rich software documentation to the PC desktop to support the new era of Microsoft Windows applications. However, WinHelp was rather cryptic, based on the RTF language and in the beginning required an extremely high level of technical knowledge to work with. This created a need for an entirely new breed of authoring tools, tools for developing software documentation, often referred to as Help Authoring Tools.

Most Help Authoring Tools were designed in the early to mid 1990's supporting early versions of Microsoft Windows. The tools were built with the best technologies of the day and did a remarkable job of taking what was originally a very technical and programmer-oriented process and not only streamlined that process, handling the code-oriented tasks behind the scenes, but also added advanced authoring capabilities. This made it possible for the professional writer or author to contribute to a very technical process with great efficiency. Instead of focusing on code related issues such as hidden footnote codes in RTF documents or scripting functions the tools allowed authors to concentrate on writing quality content and structuring that content for the best user experience. This helped to ensure that users could find the information they needed quickly and efficiently.

Over time many of the original technologies changed, and changed, and changed again. The RTF-based WinHelp led to Microsoft HTML Help, a compiled format released with Windows 98 and leveraging the newer HTML technology. RTF footnote codes and macros where replaced with ActiveX controls, JavaScript, and DHTML. Later browser-based options for delivering software documentation were developed. This allowed authors to break the Windows PC desktop barrier allowing single documentation systems to be delivered to multiple platforms such as Macintosh or Linux. These new formats could also be published on Intranets, Extranets, or even on the World Wide Web. Now we are in the latest evolutionary changes in the documentation industry. With advancements such as XML, newer programming languages, new frameworks like .NET, and modern and compliant browsers, it was time for a new authoring tool with a brand new architecture to not only accommodate these new technologies, but to leverage their strengths.

The main goal of MadCap Software is to take all of the skills we developed during the first evolutionary years in this industry and combine that knowledge with the absolute latest in available technologies, to bring the technical writing community a tool, no, an authoring platform, that will carry them many years into the future. The goal in creating MadCap Flare was to provide a modern, purpose-built, single-sourcing system that is standards compliant, XML-based, Unicode, and with a completely transparent architecture. Many may still use the phrase Help Authoring Tool, and while the concepts behind Flare can be traced back to those humble beginnings, the Flare publishing system has been designed to be much more. A system for creating software documentation, policies, procedures, knowledge bases, or any other complex documentation which you may need to create and publish.

This book will help you in exploring and learning the capabilities of the MadCap Flare publishing system and MadCap Software would like to thank the author for doing such a commendable job in teaching and explaining its many capabilities.

San Diego, January 2008

Mike Hamilton

Vice President MadCap Software

Preface

Imagine you are in a foreign city, you have an appointment, and you want to be on time. How do you get to your destination? Chances are good that you will be on time if you have a navigation device with the latest maps. Or you can buy a city map and use that to get to your destination. Maybe you take a taxi cab and have the driver bring you or you can rely on your good sense of orientation. The way the city was built may help your orientation. A city built in blocks that look like a chess board may help you to get to your destination, but a city that grew in a random, seemingly chaotic pattern may not. You may also ask at the hotel for the way. The staff will tell you about points of orientation, which may be helpful or just take you more time. Unless you call a taxi cab or use a navigation device chances are that you will get lost.

The city as "interface" can enhance or obstruct your orientation. Street signs can be easy to spot or they can be hidden. House numbers may follow the system you are used to from home or they may be organized in an entirely different way. One-way streets and left-turn restrictions may help you out on the way or result in a detour. Important buildings may or may not be signposted. You will try out different ways and strategies of orientation. As a last resort you will ask for directions. Most likely you will look for a tourist information center rather than a department store. In case you find the tourist information center you may still be disappointed: you have to wait in line, the clerk adds stories about the city's history to the directions or will send you on a especially scenic path half around the city. Depending on how important the appointment is you may give up and cancel. But when you want to find the way back to the hotel you need to persevere until you are there.

This short example shows that you can always get to a point in an unknown environment without knowing what to do next. At that point not only good navigation is needed, but also the correct information at the right place. Online help is supposed to do both. But online help is an additional system in which users need orientation and to find their way.

What is a good online help supposed to look like? What makes sense and is of use to the reader? What improves orientation and what makes it more difficult to find and absorb information? Scientists of various disciplines researched how we capture information on screen and also how we get sidetracked and confused. Linguists and especially computer linguists looked into the comprehensibility of texts, psychologists and educators researched the comprehensibility of texts and how knowledge is acquired, and ergonomists and communication specialists discussed the presentation of information. Online help systems are interdisciplinary structures.

This book brings the most important basics of creating online help systems together. It demonstrates how to generate online help systems that are optimized for the readers. Reading from screen is still uncommon as we are mainly used to reading from paper. We have become more accustomed to reading from screen due to the increasing use of computers in the workplace and also through the spread of the Internet. We have developed strategies that make searching texts on screen better. The main topic of this book is how this and other strategies need to be learned so that they can be supported using the correct presentation in online help systems.

The implementation of help systems is demonstrated using the help authoring tool Flare. Flare is currently the most modern help authoring tool available on the market. Flare also acts as a help authoring system that supports the creation of online help as well as manuals. This so called single sourcing is not covered in this book. The generation of online help is embedded in a documentation process, which itself is embedded in a development process. Ideally, both processes are geared towards the user and interact with each other: the so called "user centered engineering". This book covers this process and its methods only indirectly.

I like to thank all who supported and encouraged me while writing this book, above all thanks to my employer cognitas GmbH and the editors. The following persons helped with answering questions and providing additions for deepening and rounding off various topics: Alfred Holland, Hannemarie Kolbus, Dr. Claus Noack, Dr. Christine Platz, Mathias Rehsöft, and Evelyn Reichardt.

A Note from the Translator

Petra Thiemann wrote an outstanding book and translating it into English brings this extraordinary source of knowledge to a new audience. MadCap Software updated Flare while the translation took place. The book has been adapted to represent the capabilities of Flare V5. Some areas that were more relevant to the German audience have been rewritten to be of use for the American reader.

The translation project was a challenge that could not have been mastered without the help of many people: Wendy Krings for editing and reviewing, Petra Thiemann for answering my many questions, Sharon Burton for referring me to John Hedtke, who pointed out the difficulties of my endeavor, and Paul Pehrson for letting me know how to publish the easy way.

I also want to thank my sons Konrad and Alton for giving me the time to do this translation and for not being too upset when answering "No." to their question if I am finally done.

David Krings

Schenectady, NY

November 2009

Table of Contents

1 Terminology

Every product is supposed to be intuitive to use, especially when the product is software. User and technical writers notice over and over again that this is not the case. Intuitive usability is still far away especially with complex products.

If a product is not intuitively usable users need a manual. If the product is software then online help systems are supposed to help users out. It does not matter if the software is for an online store or the control program for a steel mill.

This chapter explains the fundamental terms used in this book and distinguishes them from each other. This book is about user-friendly online help. But is user-friendly also functional? What does ergonomics or usability mean? Are online help systems really online?

1.1 User-friendliness, Usability & Co

Usability is used as a synonym for ease of use and user-friendliness. Today the most common definition of usability is given by the standard ISO 9241 "Ergonomic requirements for office work with visual display terminals" with its 17 parts.

Part 110 of the standard defines usability as the extent to which a product can be used by specific users so that particular goals can be reached effectively, efficiently, and satisfactorily. That means that usability is not a set measure. One has to keep in mind for which purpose and for which context a specific product was designed.

The **usage context** includes factors that can influence the usability of a product, such as the users, the task, the tools, and the environment. One can rarely assume that all users have generally the same user profile, similar precognition, and a comparable educational background. The author has to at least consider the difference between novices and professionals.

For a long time the assumption was that users accessed the help only when they wanted to solve a particular problem with the product. Christian Bartsch found out from a survey of German and Italian users that this applies to a large portion of the users. However, one third of the users also accessed the online help in order to extend and deepen their existing knowledge of the product. These users do not see help systems as the last resort when peers and other sources did not help. These expert users often use online help more often and more successfully than novices. This means that technical writers need to consider the usage context. Some users seek quick answer to specific problems while others simply want to learn more about the software.

Effectivity describes the exactness and completeness of how a user reaches a specific goal. Online help is effective if a user reaches the goal. In the easiest scenario, the goal can be finding information, but it can also be the solution of a very specific problem. The more exact and complete the result, the more effective it is. The required effort is part of the efficiency.

Efficiency designates the least amount of effort that a user needs for reaching a goal. Efficiency is seen in regards to the way that leads to the solution. Therefore, online help systems should be designed as simple as possible. The relevant effort can include psychological or physical demands, time, material resources, or financial expenses.

Additionally, a user needs to be satisfied when working with online help. **Satisfaction** is reached when expectations are met or exceeded. Following the ISO standard satisfaction exists only when the expectations are exceeded.

Effectivity and efficiency can be measured objectively by watching a test user who searches for particular information and determining if everything can be found and how many steps were necessary. The last criterion for online help – satisfaction – is not measurable. One can only find out if an online help system is satisfactory by asking a test user for a subjective opinion. The following could be possible survey questions: "Did you like the help system? Did you get the impression that it was easy to find your way around? How difficult was it to find the desired information?" In order to get more representative results more than one test user has to be asked.

In conclusion, an online help system is user-friendly when a user can reach a goal (such as the solution to a specific problem) effectively, efficiently, and satisfactorily. Depending on the online help not all criteria have to be weighted equally.

User-friendliness is closely coupled with ergonomics. The standard ISO 6385:2004-05 defines ergonomics as the scientific discipline and the systematic study that deals with the explanation of the interaction between human and other elements of a system, as well as the profession that applies the theory, principles, data, and methods with the goal to optimize the comfort of the human and the performance of the entire system.

Generally, ergonomics is understood as the adjustment of tools to the musculoskeletal and cognitive system of humans, such as physical strength and operating space. Software ergonomics in particular deals with the adjustment of the software to cognitive and physical abilities or characteristics of humans. The goal of software ergonomics is the adjustment of the characteristics of a dialog system to match the characteristics of the users of the system.

Inadequate software design leads to increased aggravation, frustration, and ultimately to errors and waste of time. The psychological demand increases and the result can be headaches, flickering in front of the eyes, or stress. After extensive duration even physical ailments can occur. This is the reason why software ergonomics is a basic requirement for computer workstations. The foundation for this is defined in the ISO 9241 "Ergonomic requirements for office work with visual display terminals".

The central aspects for software design are:

- the ways of human information processing such as short term memory, metaphors, color recognition, etc.
- the tasks that the users are supposed to complete using the software
- the environment of the organization in which the task is performed (usage context)

Only under these preconditions can software be ergonomic and used well. Therefore, software ergonomics includes user and task orientation.

1.2 Online Documentation

Much of what is called "online" today is more accurately named "on screen". The term "online" was coined based on the first experiences with the Internet and means "to be connected via cable" or more specifically "to be available via Internet".

Manuals in PDF format on a CD or a local help system are not online in the purest sense of the term. Over time the term online became more common and it lends itself to be all-inclusive. The definition "in file format and displayed on screen" is plausible and is in fact used for a long time already. Defined in this way online documentation and online help are included.

Online documentation includes information that can be displayed on screen and are intended for product documentation and manuals. This definition is in line with guidelines of professional associations for technical documentation as well as the ISO/IEC 18019 "Software and system engineering – Guidelines for the design and preparation of user documentation for application software". The term "user assistance" comes closest to the definition of online documentation.

Online documentation can be split into three categories:

- user assistance
- eLearning
- user manuals on screen

Online help is in the category of user assistance and therefore is part of online documentation. The online documentation itself is part of online information.

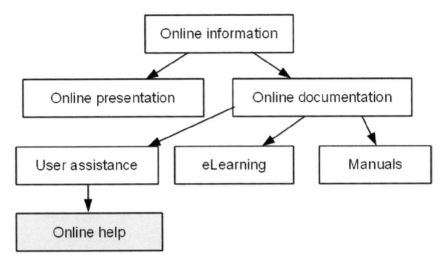

Figure 1: Categories of online information

1.2.1 User Assistance

User assistance includes all those types of information that support the user while using the application on screen. They offer selective information and help for the product. Examples are:

- labels in the user interface of the software (such as title bar, menu bar, buttons, fields)
- tool tips / bubble help
- messages
- wizards
- context sensitive help (at field or dialog level)
- context free help

User assistance is split into primary assistance and secondary assistance:

- **Primary assistance:** All types of information that are directly visible in the user interface without requiring any action of the user (for example, labels or status bar).
- **Secondary assistance:** All types of information that not directly visible and that require a user action (for example, a tool tip only shows after moving the mouse).

1.2.2 eLearning

eLearning includes all those forms of information that are intended to guide the user in using the application on screen and make access for new users easier. eLearning provides introduction and user guidance. Examples are:

- introductions without direct connection to the product (such as computer based training, web based training)
- introductions with direct connection to the product (such as tutorials)
- training videos
- product overview (such as a guided tour)

1.2.3 On screen Manuals

On screen manuals are all those forms of information that enhance or replace user assistance, eLearning, and paper based documentation and that provide a complete description of the product. They are distributed either on CD-ROM or via the Internet. Examples are e-books

- that are a replica of the printed version so that the user can print them (such as user manuals, maintenance manuals, installation manuals, mounting instructions);
- that are especially formatted for use on screen (such as process descriptions, product descriptions, user manuals).

Books are defined by a page oriented and generally linear design. Books are structured in chapters or sections and can be delivered and accessed independently from the product.

1.3 Usefulness

The usability expert Jakob Nielsen considers usability to be a sub-section of usefulness. At the same time Nielsen also differentiates between usability and utility.

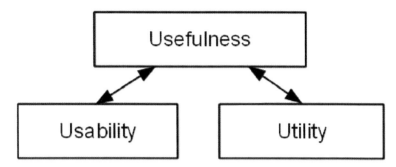

Figure 2: Categories of usefulness

A system is useful when the utility and usability enable a user to reach a specific goal without problems. The usefulness of an online help system is defined by its utility and user-friendliness. Expediency is created by adding functions to online help systems that are necessary to fulfill important goals. That means the online help system does not only have to have the suitable content, it must be locatable. Once the user found the information he or she must be able to understand and apply it.

There are a wide range of considerations when addressing the user-friendliness of an online help system: from usage context to usefulness, which are determined by the expectations of the users.

2 From Input to Output

In the 80s, Bill Gates already wished for "information at your finger tips". Although he meant mainly the World Wide Web, the same demand applies to online help because it is supposed to quickly provide the user with help for a current problem. Online help systems deliver mainly specific support and are less of a reference guide. Nevertheless, online help systems are supposed to provide a framework that enhances current knowledge.

The various information units for specific support form a network of coequal bits of information that the author has to make accessible for the user (see chapter "Navigation"). The following rule applies to online help: provide as much information as necessary to solve the current problem, but not more. Too much information is either not read or it distracts the user from the information searched for.

Online help systems are considered to be more like software than documentation. Although online help describes the graphical user interface of software it is deeply connected to the application, especially in the case of context sensitive help. Therefore, online help is considered a hybrid because on one hand help expands the common documentation, but on the other hand help is situated between the product and any other documentation.

This chapter describes the span from input to output. In the middle is the technical writer who writes the online help. Input is not only the core product description, but also the expectations of the readers as well as the various types of help. Output is the specific help format. Both influence the options that a technical writer can use for creating online help.

2.1   Expectations of the Readers

By now it is expected that many software products have a graphical user interface that makes accessing the functions easier for the users. It is further expected that the graphical user interface is described in an online help system.

Surveys show that users make use of online help only on rare occasions using it as a last resort. First users attempt to solve the problem by trial and error. Then coworkers or friends are asked for help or the World Wide Web is searched for a solution. Only after that users consult manuals or online help for support.

Studies about the reasons for this approach showed that online help has a bad reputation in general. The desired information cannot be found or searching for it is difficult. And when the information is finally found it is often not very helpful. The expectations of users in regards to online help are satisfied inadequately.

The standard ISO 9241 "Ergonomic requirements for office work with visual display terminals" puts a lot of emphasis on the user expectations. What can users expect from online help systems?

- Users want to solve their problem and find the information to do so quickly. Various search strategies and approaches need to be satisfied based on the different user behaviors.

- Once the users find the information they also want to understand it. Users expect simple wording and short, succinct text.

- Users also do not want to be left alone with abbreviations or unknown terminology. They expect an explanation within the text or in a glossary.

- Novices want more detailed information than expert users.

- The problem that users want to solve is often a specific task or goal. Therefore, users expect in online help systems descriptions of actions through task dependent instructions (directions for use or step-by-step instructions).

A technical writer needs to know the audience well in order to satisfy these expectations. This can be achieved through analysis of the target group and usage.

2.1.1 Target Group Analysis

Different target groups need different depths of information and each group requires a specific language. Something that is of great help for one group may confuse or even enrage a different group. Studies have shown that novices require more information and simpler language compared to experts. Experts as well as novices benefit from a well organized and structured text.

Various methods exist for target group analysis, for example:

- collecting existing knowledge from various departments such as marketing, support, or sales
- evaluating target group analyses from similar products or previous product versions
- interview
- questionnaire
- user test
- combination of several methods

There are different pieces of information that are considered relevant during a target group analysis.

2.1.1.1 *Determining the Characteristics*

A target group rarely has a homogeneous knowledge and experience background. Typically, the audience is made up of various groups such as novices, experienced users, and experts, which all have different previous knowledge and demands. Some sources call these groups laypersons, instructed persons, and specialists.

The previous knowledge that the user is assumed to have can be different on various levels, for example in regards to the product, the industry, the special knowledge, etc. These differences have to be determined and grouped, for example in a grid that then can be used for listing the reasonable terminology or the activity and learning behavior.

2.1.1.2 *Determining the Information Demand*

The information demand of the various groups differs in the way information is presented. Questions arise if the reader

- wants to be informed,
- wants a reference,
- wants to build up or deepen knowledge about the product, or
- wants to receive instructions.

For example, an expert does not need special learning environments or overview information that a novice does. The expert can use several points of entry into a topic and due to the previous knowledge acquisition of new knowledge requires less effort and typically yields a bigger gain.

2.1.1.3 *Allocating Reader Types*

Types of readers can be differentiated by their use and search strategies:

- A disciplined reader wants to read a lot about a topic and typically reads in a linear fashion. This type of reader is rare and does not bode well as an example. One variation of the disciplined reader is the active reader who generates his own strategies for acquiring knowledge, such as making notes or setting bookmarks.

- The undisciplined reader or wild browser has no idea how much time he will spend with reading. He reads selectively and looks for quick results, which means getting as much information as possible in the least amount of time.

- The expert looks up information and is interested in new or deeper knowledge. He has precise goals and expectations.

- The practitioner is mainly interested in transferring the theory into practice.

2.1.2 Usage Analysis

The usage analysis covers the situations in which the documentation is used, the so called usage context. The online help for a control program needs to be different than the online help for a web based store. The usage analysis helps to develop the usage scenarios that have to be supported by user-friendly online help. The broader the group of users of a product, the more difficult it is to determine usage scenarios.

One thing that can be assumed for online help is that the user is in front of a monitor. The user can sit, stand, kneel, be at a workstation with good or bad lighting, and have a lot or not much space available. This makes it difficult to find general scenarios. For a long time it was assumed that users of online help are in a problem or stress situation. The pressure to act and the related stress can only be estimated.

Surveys show that users not only use online help in stress situations, but also use online help to acquire deeper knowledge. In such a case the usage scenario is characterized by motivation and calmness of the user rather than by stress and frustration. Online help systems support the work, but are not necessary for performing the work. Online help systems support learning processes, but they are not learning software.

2.2   Types of Online Help

Depending on the project and assignment, a technical writer can be confronted with various requests for the online help. The term user assistance covers all types of online help systems that support the user while operating a software application. The following sections contain short descriptions of the various parts of user assistance. The focus of this book is on online help systems. The standard ISO 13407 "Human-centered design processes for interactive systems" determines the process of developing a software user interface.

2.2.1   Labels

The reasonable and correct labeling of a software user interface (such as a title bar, button labels, field labels) is part of the user assistance which includes online help. The closer the used terminology is to the vocabulary of concepts of the potential users the easier it is for the users to grasp the concepts of the software. The closer the labeling and the processes are to known tasks the easier it is for users to operate the software application.

The labels of a software user interface are stored in a so called resource file. The format of the resource file depends on the development framework used.

2.2.2   Tool Tips / Bubble Help

Tool tips or bubble help provide short pieces of information for an element of the user interface and are displayed when the mouse pointer moves over the element. The texts for tool tips are stored in resource files as well.

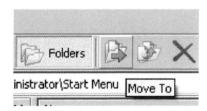

Figure 3:An example of a tool tip

2.2.3 Messages

The term "messages" covers the following message types:

- status messages are messages displayed in windows or the status bar and provide information about the condition of the hardware or software.

- confirmation messages are messages and feedback requests that appear after correct entries or commands were issued, such as security questions or approval messages.

- error messages provide information about errors caused by the system or the user.

In particular, error messages are often cryptic and not easy to understand so the user typically has no other choice than to click the OK button. Online help can offer explanations about the cause of the error and provide solutions.

The management and storage of message texts is determined by the developer and the development environment: they can either be located in resource files or implemented as context sensitive online help.

2.2.4 Wizards

A wizard is a software feature that guides the user through a complex sequence of process steps. Either the user or the software application starts the wizard. A wizard typically consists of several dialog boxes that the user completes one after another. Many wizards provide embedded help, which means that the help content is displayed directly on the dialog boxes of the wizard.

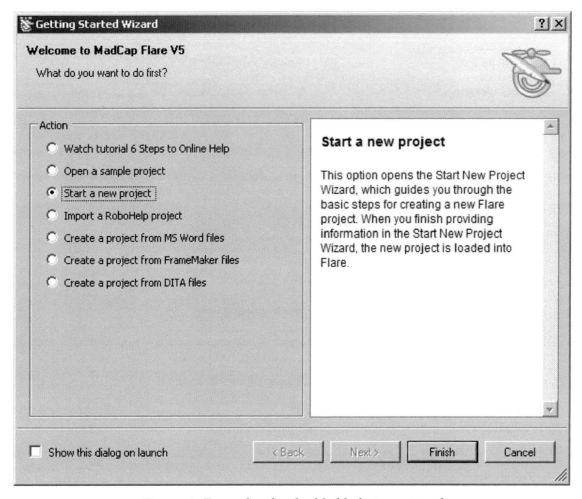

Figure 4: Example of embedded help in a wizard

2.2.5   Context sensitive Help

Context sensitive help is online help that is applicable to the current usage context, typically a dialog box or a user interface element. Context sensitive help at the element level is also called direct help. Elements can be fields, buttons, commands, etc. Online help at the element level can only provide selective and isolated help.

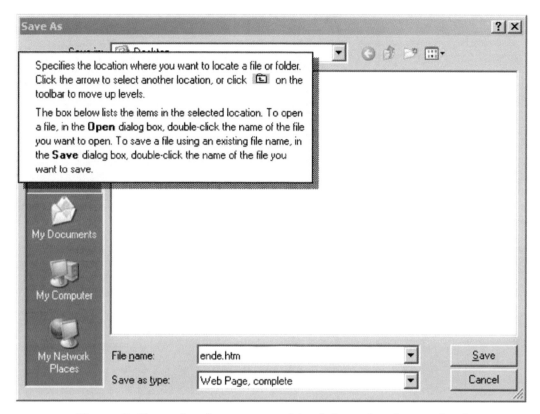

Figure 5: Example of context sensitive help at the element level

Context sensitive help at the dialog box level describes an entire dialog box, window, or tab and includes all of the user interface elements, their relationship to each other, and their dependencies. The less concept knowledge the target audience or the situation requires the more suitable context- sensitive help is at the dialog box or element level compared to context free help.

The look of context sensitive help can differ. Typical examples are: bubble help, popup help, or help windows that show online help. Context sensitive help that is displayed as part of the user interface is called embedded help.

The connection between the software application and the online help can also differ significantly. The following options exist:

- help menu in the graphical user interface: the individual menu commands open specific parts of the online help system, such as the search dialog box or the table of contents

- F1 help: pressing the F1 key on the keyboard shows the applicable information for the currently selected element or dialog box

- help button in a dialog box or the question mark button in the title bar

- dynamic help: embedded help that automatically shows the applicable information as part of the user interface for the current activity

The storage and management of help contents of context sensitive help depends on the developer and the development environment as well: the contents can be in resource files, text files, or exist as independent help system.

2.2.6 Context free Help

Context free help systems provide information about the product independently from the current use. This type of online help is usually an unconnected system that is displayed in its own window (including navigation, table of contents, topics). For further details see the section 2.3 "Help Formats and Help Windows".

Context free online help is best suited for overviews, introductions, and comprehensive processes. This type of help is usually accessed via

- the help menu in the user interface, or

- the file system.

2.2.7 Summary

The technical writer has various options to create and manage online help systems and other parts of user assistance. The following table provides an overview of the parts of user assistance. The acronym HAT stands for "help authoring tool".

Table 1: Parts of user assistance

Content	Display	Data Format
Labeling of the user interface	Graphical user interface	Depending on software: ASCII, XML
Tool tips	Graphical user interface	Depending on software: ASCII, XML
Messages	Graphical user interface	Depending on software: ASCII, XML
Online help for wizards	Graphical user interface or help window	Depending on software or HAT
Context sensitive help	Help window	Depending on HAT
Context free help	Help window	Depending on HAT

A technical writer works on three levels that influence each other:

Level 1: the product and its graphical user interface that needs to be documented

Level 2: the source format of the online help in the HAT

Level 3: the help format in the help window

2.3   Help Formats and Help Windows

Online help was introduced with the second quasi standard for graphical user interfaces: Microsoft Windows. Microsoft includes since the release of Windows 3.0 a help viewer, which is referenced here as "help window". The help compiler and a tool for creating online help (HelpWorkshop) is made available for download by Microsoft since the release of Windows 3.0. The various versions of Windows introduced different help formats and other software companies created different formats as well.

2.3.1   Winhelp

Winhelp was the first proprietary help format from Microsoft. It is a compressed .hlp file that can be run on a 16 bit Windows systems. Winhelp is supported by all Windows versions until Windows XP. Users of Windows Vista or Windows 7 who want to use Winhelp need to download an additional application from Microsoft.

Winhelp is a mature help format. Microsoft still maintains this format, but did not conduct any further development for over ten years. Although Microsoft announced the discontinuation of this format several times, many help systems are still in this format. The context sensitive connection is made with the Winhelp API, which is accessed through the user interface of the documented application.

The Winhelp window is typically a window with two display areas, one for the toolbar and one for the content. The source is one or more RTF files created in Word.

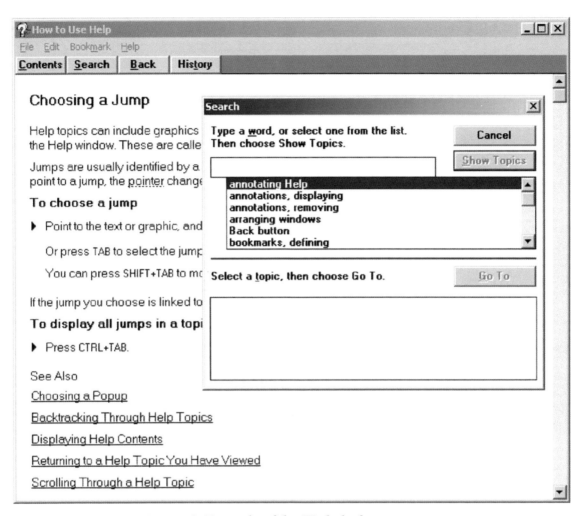

Figure 6: Example of the Winhelp format

2.3.2   HTMLHelp

HTMLHelp is the successor of Winhelp. HTMLHelp is also a proprietary help format, which can be used on 32 bit Windows platforms since Windows 98. The help format is a compressed .chm file that typically only runs on Windows systems. A requirement for the help window is Internet Explorer version 4.0 or higher.

HTMLHelp is a mature help format as well. Since a few years Microsoft only maintains HTMLHelp and no longer conducts any development for it. The context sensitive connection is made with the HTMLHelp API, which is accessed through the user interface of the documented application.

The HTMLHelp window is typically a window with three display areas, which is also called tripane. A hierarchical navigation was added to the display areas of toolbar and contents. The source files are several HTML files. MadCap Flare supports the HTMLHelp format.

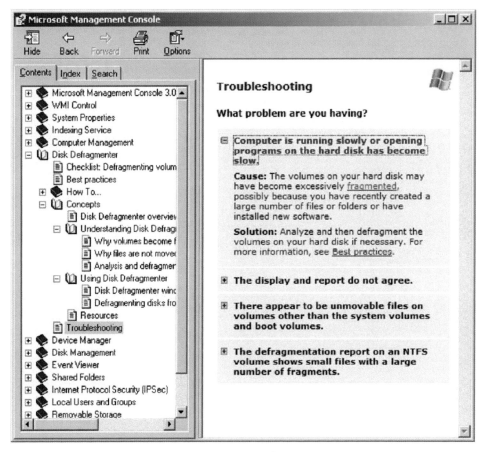

Figure 7: Example of the HTMLHelp format

2.3.3 Browser-based Help

Browser-based help is also called WebHelp and is a help format that is based on HTML. It can be displayed in any web browser on any operating system. The help format consists of several HTML files that can be viewed in a browser of one's choice. The help window works like HTMLHelp and has three display areas that are recreated using frames. MadCap Flare supports browser-based help. Browser-based help systems can run locally on a computer or be accessed globally via the Internet.

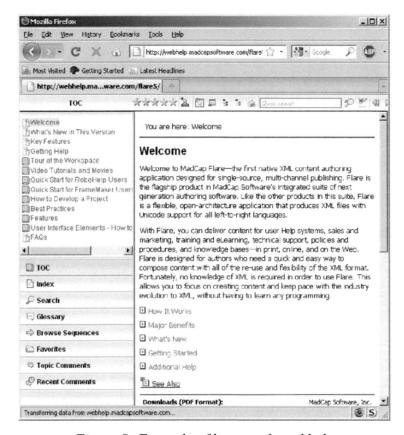

Figure 8: Example of browser-based help

2.3.3.1 *Local browser-based help*

Local browser-based help systems are platform independent and run locally on the computer of the user. The vendors of help authoring systems each have their own variation of a local browser-based help, which is called WebHelp, InterHelp, or WebworksHelp. Generally, any browser is suitable for displaying the help system.

Some software companies designed their own help formats that are considered "browser-based", because they are built upon HTML. Many of these formats require a special help viewer, which resembles a browser, but cannot be chosen freely. The help viewer is then required in order to display the help system correctly. For example, AppleHelp can be displayed with some restrictions in any browser, but that is not the case for JavaHelp. The following table compares the most popular company-specific, HTML-based help systems.

Table 2: HTML-based help formats

	DotNet Help	**JavaHelp**	**OracleHelp for Java**	**AppleHelp**
Company	MadCap Software	Sun Microsystems	Oracle Inc.	Apple
Operating system	Windows	Windows, Mac OS, Unix, Linux	Windows, Mac OS, Unix, Linux	Mac OS, Unix, Linux
Requirement	None	JRE	JVM	None
Help format	HTML files, start file .mchelp	Java archive	Java archive	HTML files
Context sensitive connection	Various APIs	JavaHelp API	JavaHelp API	AppleHelp API
Viewer	MadCap Help Viewer	Java Help Viewer	Oracle Help Viewer	AppleHelp Viewer, browser
Multilingual skins available for Viewer	Yes	No	No	No
Dynamic help	Yes	No	No	No
Support by MadCap Flare	Yes	No	No	No

Figure 9: Example of AppleHelp

2.3.3.2 *Server based help formats*

Server-based help formats are a variation of the browser-based help formats. Server-based help runs as a server application on a central computer. Multiple users can access the same version of the online help at the same time when it runs on a server. Furthermore, content is more easily updated because only one installation of the online help has to be updated. The following help formats offer a server-based version:

- JavaHelp 2.0 from Sun Microsystems

- OracleHelp for the Web from Oracle Inc.

- WebHelp Pro from Adobe Inc.

- WebHelp Plus from MadCap Software

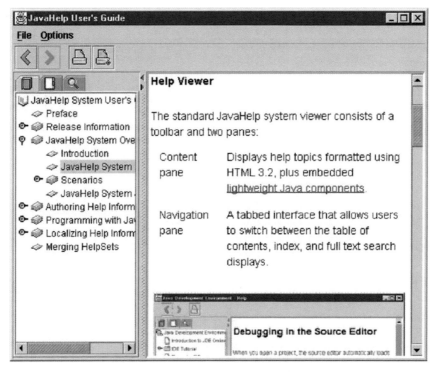

Figure 10: Example of JavaHelp

2.3.4 Vista Help

Vista Help, also known under the previous code name Longhorn Help, is a new help format that was announced by Microsoft several years ago, but the release was delayed several times. Originally, the release was planned to coincide with the release of the Windows Vista operating system.

Windows Vista has been released and official announcements by Microsoft indicate that the new help format will not be available for the next version. Microsoft wants to use the help format exclusively for their own application and further test it. This means that technical writers need to rely on HTMLHelp, which will be the standard for online help for a long time on Windows systems.

2.3.5   Help Viewers

The help window is a part of the help viewer and displays the generated online help. The various operating systems and help formats use different help viewers. The look of each help window can be changed and depends on the help format. The following table shows an overview of the most important help viewers.

Table 3: Help viewers for different operating systems

Operating System	WinHelp	HTMLHelp	WebHelp	DotNet Help	JavaHelp	Oracle Help for Java
Windows 3.1	Integrated into OS	Not available	Browser	Not available	JavaViewer	Oracle Viewer
Windows 95, NT	Integrated into OS	Internet Explorer	Browser	Not available	JavaViewer	Oracle Viewer
Windows 98, 2000, XP, 2003	Integrated into OS	Internet Explorer	Browser	MadCap Viewer	JavaViewer	Oracle Viewer
Windows Vista	external	Internet Explorer	Browser	MadCap Viewer	JavaViewer	Oracle Viewer
Apple Macintosh	external	external	Browser	Not available	JavaViewer	Oracle Viewer
Unix, Linux	external	external	Browser	Not available	JavaViewer	Oracle Viewer

2.4   Help Project

The sources of an online help system consist of several files and are integrated in a help project. A help project consists of at least the following files:

- project file
- topic files
- table of contents file

- layout template file

- depending on the help authoring tool used further control files, such as target definition files, master page files, glossary files

- for context sensitive help also a header file and an alias file that are used for the connection of the online help with the individual elements and dialog boxes of the graphical user interface

2.5 Compiling Online Help

Only compiling, building, or generating makes an executable help system out of the individual HTML and control files in a help project. The index and the full text search are also generated during compiling.

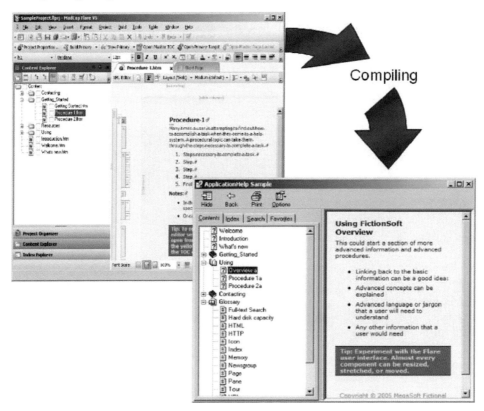

Figure 11: Compiling online help

3 The Help Authoring Tool Flare

Flare is a help authoring tool from MadCap Software that is used for demonstrating the implementation of the typical elements of an online help system. This chapter will provide a short introduction into the organization of Flare. This chapter is not intended as Flare documentation. For detailed information consult the online help of Flare.

Flare is now in its fifth version on the market and offers, besides many new approaches, an impressive amount of functionality for the creation of online help systems. Flare is designed as a help authoring tool, but it can also be used for generating all kinds of documentation that can be displayed on screen. This does not have to be a help system, but can also be web pages or knowledge bases for use in an Intranet or for call centers.

Flare is based on XML and offers its own XML editor with WYSIWYG mode (what you see is what you get). XML based means that all files of a Flare project, such as content and control files, are stored in XML format (no proprietary tags). This allows for an easier exchange of contents. The XML format can easily be used with source control or version control systems as well as translation management tools (translation memory). Flare offers connections for both application types.

For now, all files within a Flare project are validated against XHTML. DITA is available since Flare V5. Other schemata or docbook adaptations cannot be used with Flare at the moment.

Flare can generate the following help formats:

- HTMLHelp
- WebHelp
- DotNetHelp

DotNetHelp

MadCap Software developed DotNetHelp specially for Microsoft Visual Studio 2005 developers and provides the MadCap help viewer that can be freely distributed. DotNetHelp contains special control elements for Visual Studio 2005 to be used for context sensitive connection. Different APIs are used depending on the type of context sensitive connection:

- HelpViewerClient API

- HelpViewerEmbeddedClient API

- IEmbeddedHelpSystem

- ICSHIDProvider API

3.1 Overview of the Graphical User Interface

Flare starts up with the main window that is segmented into three main areas:

- hierarchical navigation (left side)

- workspace (middle)

- dialog box for special tasks (right side)

3.1.1 The Main Window of Flare

Starting from the top, the main window of Flare has the following sections:

- title bar showing the name of the currently opened project

- menu bar in which all commands for editing are organized in menus

- general toolbar showing the most important commands as icons

- toolbar for text formatting (can be turned off)

Title bar

Menu bar

Tool bar

Local tool bars

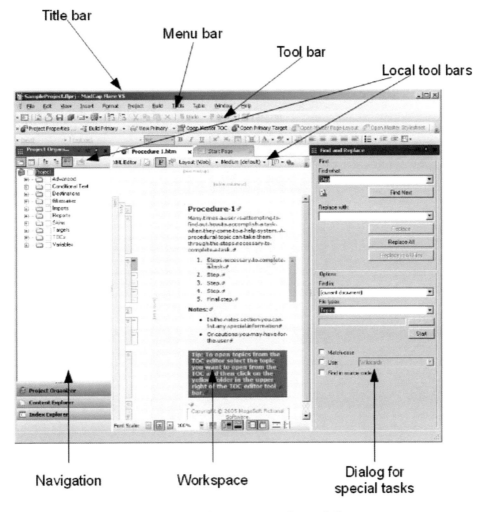

Navigation   Workspace   Dialog for
                                       special tasks

Figure 12: The main window of Flare

3.1.2   Editors

All files of a Flare project can be edited in the specific editors, for example a stylesheet is edited in the stylesheet editor. Each file is opened by double-clicking and remains open until it is closed explicitly. Changed files are marked with an asterisk in the tab header. Flare asks if a changed file is to be saved when closing it, which also allows closing the file without saving the changes.

- The menu command **File** > **Save All** saves all files that are currently open.

- The menu command **Window** > **Close All Documents** closes all files that are currently open.

The editors typically provide an additional toolbar with relevant commands for the object currently worked on.

The most important editor is the XML editor for the help contents. XML knowledge is not required as the XML operations are all done in the background. Those who do know XML can have the tags displayed and manipulate them.

3.1.2.1 Display of XML Structure

The XML structure of a topic can be displayed with the following icons in the local toolbar:

turns the display of the structure tags on or off

turns the display of DIV and SPAN tags on or off

The same applies for the structure of a table that can be displayed with the following icons in the local toolbar:

turns the display of the rows of a table on or off

turns the display of the columns of a table on or off

Each XML tag can be edited within the text or the structural display via context menus. The context menus open when clicking on a tag with the right mouse button.

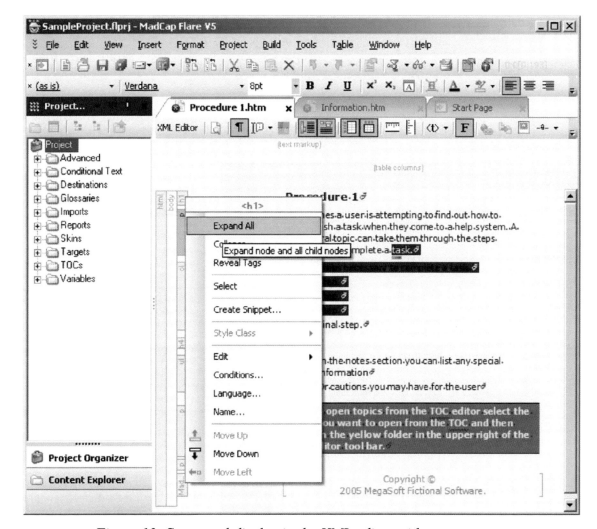

Figure 13: Structural display in the XML editor with context menu

The context menu for a particular XML tag can be opened directly from the text as well. Every XML tag shows an orange marker when the tag is clicked on or the mouse pointer hovers over it. This applies to paragraph tags as well as span tags. Clicking on the orange marker opens the context menu with the applicable commands for this tag.

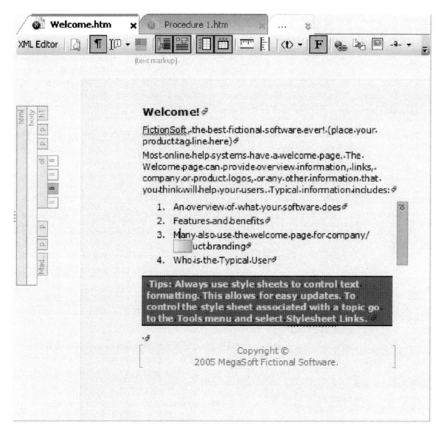

Figure 14: Marker for XML tag within the text

Cursor formats within the text

The cursor can change to the following formats while working in the editor:

[marks the start of an XML tag

]   marks the end of an XML tag

| indicates that the cursor is within one or between two XML tags

Markers

Flare controls topic functions through markers. The following markers can be found:

XML tag

·FictionSoft·	SPAN tag
Preview	Index key word
⚲	Bookmark or named element
Topic Area	Concept
·LongTime: 10:46:59·	Variable
See Also	See Also link

The menu command **View > Show > Show Markers** allows toggling the display of markers. The command **View > Show > Marker Width** allows changing the display of the markers within a topic.

3.1.3 Explorers

The explorers appear in the area of the navigation and provide an overview of specific parts of the help projects. The most important explorer is the **Content Explorer**, which contains all topics of the project and also the topic related control files, which are stored in the Resources folder. The **Project Organizer** is also part of the navigation and provides access to all project related control files.

3.2 The Flare Project at the File Level

Flare manages all parts of a help project at file level. The structure represents that of the graphical user interface. When nothing else is defined Flare stores all projects in the folder `C:\Documents and Settings\<user name>\My Documents\My Projects`.

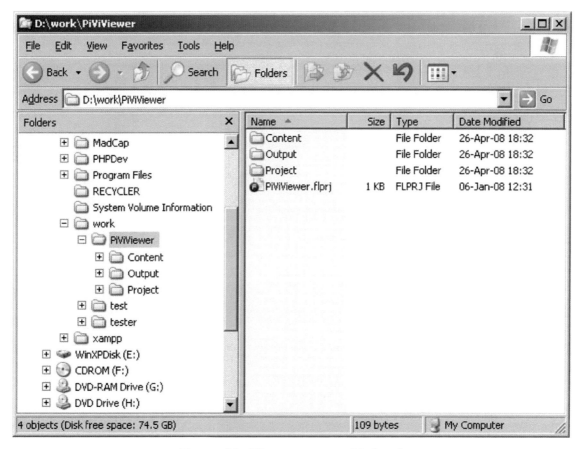

Figure 15: Flare project at file level

Flare creates a folder for each project. This folder contains the project file (file extension .flprj) and the following folders:

- Content for the topics and topic related control files

- Project for the project related control files

- Output for the various output formats

The structure at file level is the same as the one used in the graphical user interface of Flare, which makes locating files easier. The only exception is the Output folder in which the compiled help formats are sorted by user name and then by type.

3.3 *Formatting within this book*

This book will format references to elements in the graphical user interface of Flare and in the file system as follows:

Table 4: Formatting within this book

Formatting	Meaning
bold	References all elements in the graphical user interface
`fixed width font`	References all elements on file system level
menu > command	Describes the menu path and the command
<styleclass>	Indicates a variable entry that depends on the project or system
CAPS	Specifies an XHTML tag, such as the XREF tag

3.4 *Customize Flare*

Flare is a complex tool that needs to fulfill many requests and expectations. Flare also tries to support various work flows. For example, most commands can be executed through various means:

- menus
- icons in the general or local toolbar
- keyboard shortcuts
- context menus for user interface elements that can be right-clicked on

Part of the user friendliness of software is that the software adjusts to the needs of the users. That applies especially for help authoring tools. Flare offers various ways to customize the user interface. Following are just two of the available options described:

- change the user interface language
- customize the window layout

3.4.1   Language of the User Interface

The Flare user interface is available in four languages. The user interface is displayed in the language that is listed at the top of the language list. The order can be changed as follows:

1. Select the menu command **Tools > Options**. The Options window appears.

2. Select the option **Show Select UI Language Dialog on Startup** by checking the check box.

3. Confirm the selection by clicking **OK**. Upon restart of Flare the following dialog box appears:

Figure 16: Select UI Language Dialog Box

4. Select the desired user interface language in the list and use the **Up** button to move it to the top of the list. Click **OK** to continue.

3.4.2   Window Layout

The Flare work environment can be customized. Any window can be dragged to a desired spot or individual windows can be hidden. Once the work environment is properly customized the settings can be saved and reloaded when needed. The following paragraphs describe the flexible customization for the various windows.

Freely position windows

In order to freely position a window that is currently displayed as a tab in the work space follow these steps:

1. Bring the window or the topic up front by clicking on the tab header.

2. Select from the **Window** menu the command **Floating**. This command is also available from the context menu that appears when right-clicking on the tab header. The window is removed from the tab and can now be dragged to any position on the screen. The command **Floating** works like a switch that toggles between tab display and floating window. In order to place the window back into the editor as a tab, select the command **Floating** from the context menu. This way you can position topics side by side and work on them in parallel.

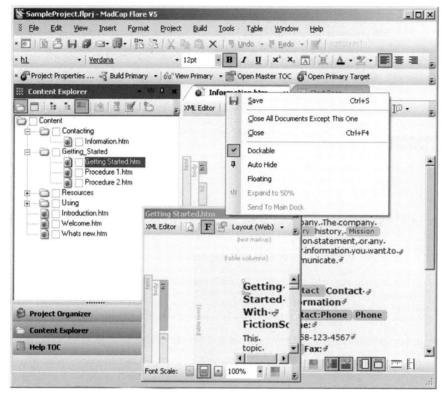

Figure 17: Positioning windows

Icons for Window Control

All other windows of Flare can also be positioned freely or hidden. The windows can be controlled through the following icons:

▦ moves the window

▾ opens the menu for the window control

½ increases or decreases the window size by 50%

⌷ hides the window automatically and displays it as toolbar at the side of the main window of Flare; moving the mouse pointer over the toolbar shows the window in its original size

✖ closes the window

Configuration of the Work Environment

The work environment can be configured through the commands in the sub-menu of **Windows > Layouts**.

3.5 Flare Project

A Flare project consists of at least the following files:

- project file: file extension .flprj
- topic files: file extension .htm
- table of contents file: file extension .fltoc within the project, file name in output is toc.xml
- index file: file name in output is index.xml
- file with cascading stylesheet: file extension .css
- target file for output: file extension .fltar
- a header file (file extension .h) and an alias file (file extension .flali) for the context sensitive connection between the online help and the elements or dialog boxes of the graphical user interface

A Flare project can contain more than just one help project. It is possible to maintain various help systems for a product in a Flare project, or maintain the online help as well as the manual. The Flare project provides the framework and the control options to create the desired output from the various topics.

Flare is more than just a help authoring tool, it offers many Content Management System (CMS) functions through Single Sourcing. The goal of this concept is to keep all contents in one source and generate from that all desired outputs.

3.5.1 Targets

A target includes the central control file for an output format. All settings that are to be applied to the output have to be defined in the target. See also section 5.7.4 "How Everything Comes Together: The Target".

A target defines,

- which output format is generated (a help format or printed output),
- what is to be included in the output (content, mainly topics),
- how the output is to be generated (layout).

3.5.2 Input Formats

Not every help project is about an entirely new product so there may also be interest in importing existing documents. Flare can use the following formats as input:

- RoboHelp projects (file extension .mpj or .xpj)
- HTMLHelp projects (file extension .hhp)
- HTML files (file extension .htm or .html)
- Word documents (file extension .doc, .docx, or .rtf)
- FrameMaker files and books (file extension .fm, .mif, or .book)
- DITA files (file extension .ditamap or .dita)

3.5.3 Output Formats

Flare offers various output formats that not only include online help formats, but also print formats. Flare can generate the following output formats:

- cross-browser, cross-platform WebHelp or WebHelp Plus
- WebHelp AIR

- HTML Help

- DotNet Help

- FrameMaker files and books

- PDF

- Word documents

- XPS files

- DITA files

3.5.4   CMS Functions

All CMS functions are integrated into the project organization. A table of contents allows specifying which contents are included and in which sequence they appear. Conditions allow excluding specific content for each target and each target can have its own layout and skin. There are also sets of variables through which changeable text portions can be managed and updated.

3.6   First Steps

This section contains an overview of the necessary steps for creating online help. The individual topics are covered in more detail in the upcoming chapters. The first steps are

- creating a project

- working within the project

- generating online help

3.6.1   Creating a Project

Flare offers various means to create a new project and add content. A project can be created by:

- adding an empty project and entering or importing contents

- adding a project through import of an existing project, which applies to HTMLHelp and RoboHelp projects

- adding a project through import of a Word or FrameMaker file

Flare provides the **Start New Project Wizard** to assist with creating a new project.

3.6.1.1 *Creating a new (empty) project*

1. Select the command **File > New Project**. The **Start New Project Wizard** appears showing the first dialog box.

2. Specify the **Project Name** and the **Project Folder** in which the project files are to be stored.

3. In case you use a source control system such as Microsoft Visual SourceSafe you can choose the option **Bind to Source Control**.

4. Click **Next** and the dialog box **Select a language...** appears.

5. Choose the language for the Flare project. This setting can be changed in the target settings if the project applies to multiple languages.

6. Click **Next** and the dialog box **Select a project template...** appears.

7. Select your own template or keep the default settings and click **Next**. The dialog box **Select a primary target...** appears.

8. Select the primary target that is to be used as a default for generating the output.

9. Click **Finish**. The project gets created and contains the following files:

Table 5: Files in a new Flare Project

File	Name	Location with the project
Topic file	Topic.htm	Topic Explorer / Content
Stylesheet	Styles.css	Topic Explorer / Resources / Stylesheets

File	Name	Location with the project
Context sensitive connection	MyAliasFile MyHeaderFile.h	Project Organizer / Advanced
Conditions	Default	Project Organizer / Conditional Text
Destination	MyDestination	Project Organizer / Destinations
Glossary	MyGlossary	Project Organizer / Glossaries
Skin	Default	Project Organizer / Skins
Target	Depending on the previously selected target type; the possibilities are: MyDotNetHelp MyFrameMaker MyHTMLHelp MyPDF MyWebHelp MyWebHelpAIR MyWebHelpPlus MyMSWord MyXHTMLBook MyXPS AIR DITA	
Table of contents	Master(Master)	Project Organizer / TOCs
Variable Set	MyVariables	Project Organizer / Variables

3.6.1.2 *Importing an existing project*

1. Select the menu command **File > Import Project > Import (Non-Flare) Project...** and the **Import Project Wizard** appears.

2. Click on the ellipsis button (**...**) next to the text field **Project file**.

3. The dialog box **Open** appears. Select the folder with the project file from the **Look in** drop-down list and enter the project file name into **File name**. The following project types can be selected:

- file extension .xpj: RoboHelp Version X5

- file extension .mpj: RoboHelp Version X4

- file extension: .hhp: HTMLHelp project

4. Click on **Open**, the dialog box closes, and the path and file name of the help project is placed into **Project file**.

5. Click **Next** to see the next dialog box.

6. Enter the name of the new project into **Project name** and select a folder for the new project in **Project folder**.

7. Click **Next** and the dialog box **Import Options** appears.

8. Select the option **Convert all topics at once** to have all topics converted to XHTML during import. If this option is not selected the conversion will take place when the topic is opened in Flare for the first time. Selecting this option is recommended.

9. Click **Next** and the dialog box **Select the Flare project language** appears.

10. Choose the language for the Flare project. This setting can be changed in the target settings if the project applies to multiple languages.

11. Click **Finish** so that the non-Flare project is converted into a new Flare project. The new project is opened in Flare automatically. In addition to the files in a new project, Flare may create the following files in these possible locations:

Table 6: Files created through import

File	Location in help project
Topic files	Content Explorer / Content
Image files	Content Explorer / Resources / Images
Master page	Content Explorer / Resources / MasterPages
Sensitive elements	Content Explorer / Resources / CHMSupport

3.6.1.3 *Importing a FrameMaker or Word file*

The following section describes an example of how to import existing contents into Flare. It is recommended for both Word and FrameMaker files that unneeded contents are removed prior to import. Unneeded contents are those contents that will be added through Flare at a later point or that are irrelevant for online help. Some examples of these unneeded contents are:

- title page
- table of contents
- page numbers
- page footers
- page headers
- numbering of headings
- image and table captions
- index

A Word or FrameMaker file can be imported into an existing project or the import can create a new project. The import of Word and FrameMaker files is similar, any differences are noted.

Importing Word files

Follow these steps to create a new Flare project by importing a Word document:

1. Select the menu command **File > Import Project > Import MS Word Documents...** and the **Import Microsoft Word Wizard** appears.
2. Click **Next** in the first dialog box. The second dialog box opens from where the Word file for the import can be selected.
3. Click on **Add Files...** and the **Open** dialog box appears.
4. Select the folder and Word file(s) for import.

5. Click **Open** and the selected file(s) are added to the **MS Word Files** list shown in the wizard.

6. Deselect the option **Link Generated Files To Source Files**. This option is only of interest when Word is to be used as an editor for the document.

7. Click on **Next**. After scanning the import file, the next dialog box of the wizard appears.

8. Select a folder for the new project and enter a project name.

9. Click on **Next** and the dialog box **'New Topic' Styles...** appears. This dialog box allows for selecting the styles that indicate a new topic, for example, headings.

10. Select the desired styles from **Used Word Styles** and click on >>> to have them added to the **'New Topic' Styles** list.

11. Click **Next** so that the next dialog box of the wizard appears. This dialog box allows setting options for splitting topics depending on their length.

12. Select the option **Avoid Creating 'Empty' Topics**. When importing a FrameMaker file additional options are available that allow specifying how to handle text and images in anchored frames:

   • The option **Generate Images for Anchored Frames when needed** instructs Flare to generate an image from an anchored frame when the frame contains text.

   • The option **Preserve Image Size** keeps the size settings for an image while importing the image with the original dimensions.

13. Click **Next** and the dialog box **Stylesheet** appears. This dialog box offers the options to either preserve the formatting or to use the standard formatting from Flare's default stylesheet. It is not recommended to preserve the formatting when importing a Word document. When importing FrameMaker files it is possible to choose the option

Conversion Styles which will open the **Import Styles Editor** in which each style can be edited before converting the file.

14. Click **Next** and the dialog box **Paragraph Style Mapping...** appears. This dialog box allows for mapping the styles from the import file to styles in Flare.

15. First select a style from the **MS Word Style** list and then select the corresponding style from the **Flarc Styles** list.

16. Click on **Map** to have the Flare style mapped with the selected style in the **MS Word Styles** list.

17. Map other styles accordingly and click on **Next**. The next dialog box is **Character Style Mapping...** and allows for mapping character level styles.

18. First select a style from the **MS Word Style** list and then select the corresponding style from the **Flare Styles** list.

19. Click on **Map** to have the Flare style mapped with the selected style in the **MS Word Styles** list. Map other styles accordingly.

    a) When importing a FrameMaker file click **Next** and the dialog box **X-Ref Style Mapping...** appears. This dialog box allows mapping the XHTML cross-reference formats with the FrameMaker cross-reference formats so that they are converted properly during the import.

    b) First select the FrameMaker format from the **FrameMaker Style** list, then select the desired XHTML format from the **Flare Styles** list.

    c) Click on **Map** and the the Flare style is added to the **Flare Style** list on the left next to the corresponding FrameMaker style.

20. Click on **Finish**. The source file is imported and split into topics. The result is shown as a preview in the **Accept Imported Documents** dialog box.

21. Click **Cancel** if corrections are needed and click **Back** to return to previous steps in order to change options.

22. Click **Accept** to complete the import with the selected settings. The new project is created and opened. A copy of the parameters is stored in the **Project Organizer** under the folder **Imports**. Besides the files for a new project Flare added files to these locations during the import:

Table 7: Files created during import

File	Location in the help project
Topic files	Content Explorer / Content
Image files	Content Explorer / Resources / Images

3.6.1.4 *Importing DITA Document Set*

The Darwin Information Typing Architecture (DITA) is an XML based documentation architecture that focuses on modular creation of information content. DITA was designed to allow a standardized exchange of documentation between diversc systems. DITA is based on three topic classes (also see 4.3 "Topic Classes"):

- concept
- task
- reference

DITA topics are extensively cross-referenced and typically include a lot of meta data that helps with searching for content.

Follow these steps to create a new Flare project by importing a DITA document set:

1. Select the menu command **File > Import Project > Import DITA Document Set...** and the **Import DITA Wizard** appears.

2. Click **Next** in the first dialog box. The second dialog box opens from where the DITA document set for the import can be selected.

3. Click on **Add Files...** and the **Open** dialog box appears.

4. Select the folder and DITA document set for import.

5. Click **Open** and the selected file(s) are added to the **DITA Files** list shown in the wizard.

6. Deselect the option **Link Generated Files To Source Files**. This option is only of interest when an editor other than Flare is to be used as an editor for the document.

7. Click on **Next**. After scanning the import file the next dialog box of the wizard appears.

8. Select a folder for the new project and enter a project name.

9. Click on **Next** and the dialog box **'Import DITA Documents...** appears. This dialog box allows for selecting the scope of the import, if an auto-reimport is supposed to happen before generating output, and if ID attributes for elements are to be preserved.

10. Make the desired selections and click **Finish**.

11. The import process starts and when it is finished the **Accept Imported Documents** wizard appears. Evaluate the preview and when the result is satisfying click **Accept**.

12. Flare creates the new project and opens it for editing.

The imported document set can be worked on the same way as with any other Flare project and may also be used to create a new DITA document set through an applicable target (see section 5.7.4 "How Everything Comes Together: The Target").

3.6.2   Working within a Help Project

Generally, every help project contains:

- topic files or other content files, e. g. glossary, snippets, images

- control files that specify how the contents are generated, e. g. ToC, target, variables, conditions

Both file types can be created, edited, deleted, and linked to each other. The editing of help topics is covered in section 4 "Topics". The most important control files are explained in sections 5 "Layout" and 6 "Navigation".

3.6.3 Generating Online Help

The generation of online help is started through a target. After importing a previous project, a Word document, or a FrameMaker file it is possible to generate online help right away. When starting with a new project at least one topic and a table of contents that includes this topic are needed.

Follow these steps to generate online help:

1. Open the **Project Organizer**.

2. Open the folder **Targets**.

3. Open the desired target with a double-click (see also section 5.7.4 "How Everything Comes Together: The Target").

4. Select the start topic on the **Basic** tab. The start topic is the topic that is opened by default when the help is opened without context-sensitivity (for example from a Help menu).

5. If desired, select an option from **Skin**.

6. Select an option from **Master TOC**.

7. Specify **Output File** and **Output Folder** if needed.

8. Select on the tab **Advanced** a **Master Page** if desired and make selections on the **Glossary** tab if needed.

9. Save the target through the menu command **File > Save**.

10. Right-click on the target in the **Project Organizer** and select **Build** (followed by the target name) from the context menu. The online help is built and saved in the designated folder. A status windows shows the progress of the generation and reports any errors.

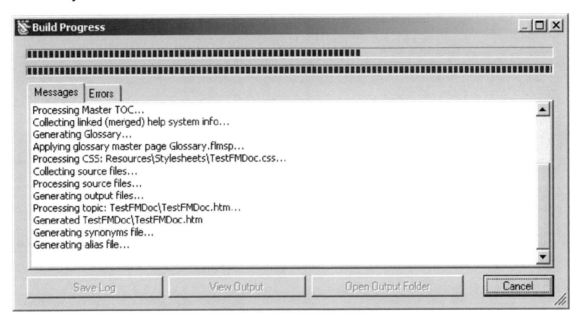

Figure 18: Build Progress

11. Click on **View Output** to see the generated help file.

Errors that occurred during generation can be saved in a log file. The saved log is stored with a date and time stamp in the folder **Reports** in the **Project Organizer**. Double-click on the log file to open it. Double-click on a listed topic to open the topic file and make the necessary edits.

Using the Preview

While working on an online help project it is not necessary to always generate the target output in order to see how changes will look. Click on ![icon] in the local toolbar of the XML editor to see the preview for the current topic.

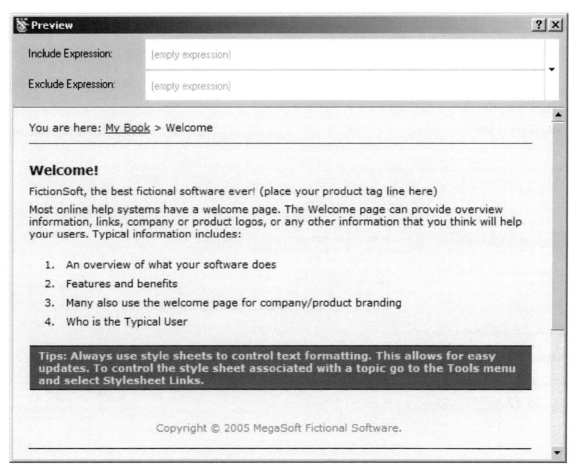

Figure 19: A preview of a topic

4 Topics

In online help, text is the medium of choice for communicating with the reader. The communication context is special because supportive tools such as inflection and gesture are missing that can help make the message clear. Additionally, the typically linear text is broken up into individual units of information that are networked together.

Online help systems are part of the entire product documentation. Ideally, contents of online help complement the other documentation so that all documentation builds a meaningful collection with only a few redundancies.

This chapter shows the connection between product information and individual topics. It describes the various types of text and presents the strategies to structure these texts and separate them into individual topic classes.

4.1 Text

Text has a practical meaning and is embedded in a communication context. It has a function and a purpose and is considered a linguistic action. Linguists describe texts with the following criteria.

Cohesion	Grammatical and lexical dependence of components
Coherence	Concepts and relationships (context)
Intentionality	Intention of the author
Acceptability	Attitude of the reader
Situationality	Meaning in a specific situation
Informativity	Expectations and level of familiarity
Intertextuality	Relationship to other texts

Writing and reading texts is communication with time delay. A user reads a text in the scope of a larger activity context, which defines the goal of the reading. Therefore, intentionality does not only exist for the author, but also for the reader. The reader expects a cohesive and coherent text, that is useful and relevant, for example, when expanding knowledge or solving a problem.

For a text to fulfill the communicative purpose it has to be not only understandable, but also correct. Correct means that it provides accurate and complete information in the scope of technical documentation, which is achieved through a review phase in the production process. Texts can be structured and presented differently. Texts are grouped into linear text and hypertext.

4.1.1 Linear Text

In a linear text the individual units of information are arranged like a string of pearls. One unit of information transitions into the next unit and alternative paths are not planned for. The most common example for a linear text is a book, which consists of chapters and paragraphs.

Technical documentation can be defined as "quasi linear": although the documents have a linear structure they are not used that way. For example, when making use of content tables, indices, overviews, cross-links, etc. Exceptions are encyclopedias, which are structured modularly.

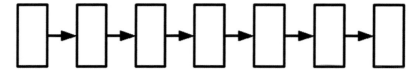

Figure 20: Linear text

4.1.2 Hypertext

Online help systems are hypertexts. A hypertext contains units of information or nodes that can be cross-linked and nested in many ways. Hypertext does not have the linear structure of a book. A network structure is created, which is not transparent to the user. The degree of nesting is different in the various systems. In some cases one can choose the paths while in other cases the paths are mainly determined by the system.

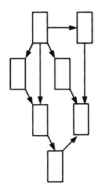

Figure 21: Hypertext

Generally, logical connections can be created in hypertexts through hyperlinks from one position in the text, the so called anchor, to any other desired position in the same text or a different document. These links are presented most of the time as either graphical buttons or colored text segments.

The hyperlinks do not necessarily point to other texts, but they can also link to pictures, graphs, animations, audio clips, or videos. This way various kinds of media can be integrated into online help. This is also referred to as hypermedia.

The single information units in a hypertext are called nodes. Similarly, how a book is made up of chapters and paragraphs a hypertext is made up of nodes, which are connected through electronic links. In online help, the node is called a topic. Both terms are used synonymously in this context.

Hypertexts can become very complex as one can see with the World Wide Web. The most diverse documents are interconnected. The user can search for information based on personal needs and can extend knowledge in those areas, where it is necessary for individual understanding and personal interests. This is a constructivist approach where each person creates an individualized world. Perception, that is based on the background of existing knowledge constructs, is interpreted and formed.

Important considerations with hypertexts are coherence and cohesion. Information is broken down into units of information that are too deep or not deep enough. Contents are often so much broken down into pieces, that it is difficult for the reader to create the relationship between the bits and pieces. The readers cannot concentrate on reading the content because the many links are distracting.

On the one hand, the reader may have to click on all the links to compile the information bit by bit in order to read the entire section. More effort is spent on navigating through the system than on reading and learning. On the other hand, the reader may forget that it is a hypertext when the information units are too large. The reader is becoming less and less active over time while reading the pages because it takes so long to read each of them.

4.2   Structural Methods

How can information be broken down and structured in a meaningful way? Three methods of structuring are known in the realm of technical communication. The methods break down and structure information under various aspects:

- Information Mapping®
- Function design
- Information design

4.2.1   Information Mapping®

Information Mapping® was designed by the psychologist Robert E. Horn. The starting points for Horn were the findings about the function principle and information processing of the human brain. The goal is to create structured texts that are easy to read and thus facilitate access to selective information.

Horn devised seven fundamental principles:

- group content into manageable pieces

- put relevant information together in one unit

- label each unit properly as this enhances the relationship between caption and content

- treat similar elements with consistency

- consider the information carriers such as text, tables, pictures, and diagrams to be equivalent

- make details accessible in the places where they are needed

- structure content hierarchically

Information Mapping® provides six information types that are used as criteria for structuring information content:

- term defines an object

- fact defines a property of an object

- principle describes a rule

- procedure describes and activity

- process describes the functionality of an object

- structure describes the composition of an object

At the start, each piece of information is associated with an information type. For example, metaphors, examples, and counter examples belong to the information type "term"; warnings, goal definitions, and requirements belong to the information type "principles". After that text is written for each information type. The text should consist of five to nine equivalent information carriers such as tables, diagrams, and so on. The choice of information carrier depends on the audience and the type of presentation, which supports the inherent logic in the best way possible.

Finally, the texts are combined into the information units block and map, and receive a caption, which explains the relationship between title and content.

The classification based on the criteria is not always distinct and the author sometimes has to decide between two information types. The interesting aspect is that information carriers such as tables, lists, and diagrams are equivalent to text, and that the corresponding information type acts as an additional level of description above the information carriers.

4.2.2   Function Design

Muthig and Schäflein-Armbruster created the function design especially for technical communication. The speech act theory and communication analysis consider communication as rule based, linguistic actions. Based on this, function design defines a variable amount of functional elements for four structural levels:

- information product
- sequence pattern
- functional unit
- markup tag

The product knowledge is split at the top level into information products, such as user manuals, service handbooks, or online help systems. The most important criteria are the audience and the point in time when the information is needed. Information products consist of sequence patterns, each of which contain a limited amount of functional units. An information product is only allowed to have specific sequence patterns.

Functional units can be goal definitions, prerequisites, activity requests, results, or basic texts and cross-references. The function design is not only a structuring method, but also a writing method. Each functional unit has set rules for wording and layout. The allowed sequence of functional units is defined in the sequence patterns.

For example, the sequence pattern "task instructions" is defined as such as that it has to begin with a "goal definition", which optionally can be followed by the functional unit "Prerequisite" and the sequence pattern "Warning". This is followed by the functional unit "Activity Request", which can be followed by the functional unit "Result" if needed. This means that the position of functional units is defined by the text structure, which typically places the units sequentially.

This structuring method improves the consistency during writing. The lowest level of the function design are markup tags, which mark up individual words or phrases.

4.2.3   Information Design

Information design is a company specific development that references Information Mapping®️ and function design systematically to each other. Pieces of information are split into information classes (comparable with the information types in Information Mapping®️), which contain function-oriented sections.

The information design defines five classes of information, which each describe equal information content with the same internal structure:

- components
- objects
- processes
- approaches
- functions

Every information class defines a specific amount of key sections in a set sequence. The information class "approach", for example, consists of the obligatory key sections "title" and "approach". Optionally, sections "prerequisite", "advice", and "warning" can be added.

In information design key sections are defined first on the basis of analysis of existing documentation and the requirements of the audience. The individual sections are then combined to target group specific documents. After that, the new documents are analyzed based on common content criteria so that they can be associated with an information class.

4.2.4 Types of Text

Independent of being linear or networked, two types of text developed in technical documentation that match the described structuring methods:

- description
- instruction

Description

Descriptive texts inform the user about fundamental issues and provide background information. Descriptions provide knowledge about contexts and the graphical user interface and its elements. Examples for predominantly descriptive texts are:

- introduction into a topic
- functional description
- user interface description

Instruction

Instructive texts intend to provide solutions that allow the user to immediately continue working with the product. Instructions provide information that applies directly to the activities of the user and illustrate possible approaches and procedures. An instructive text prompts the reader to do something. Examples for predominantly instructive texts are:

- service manual
- implementation manual
- operations instruction

An instructive text always has to provide the progression of the steps in that sequence in which the tasks are to be completed. Steps or intermediate steps are not allowed to be missing. The activity instruction should not contain general descriptions, but only the precise steps.

4.2.5   Darwin Information Typing Architecture (DITA)

The Darwin Information Typing Architecture (DITA) is a set of Document Type Definitions (DTD) for XML and conventions for creating technical documentation. DITA was developed by a workgroup at IBM that was looking for new way to author the large amounts of technical documentation needed at IBM. Although IBM already had a scheme in place to support the documentation needs it no longer really addressed the needs of technical documentation. The workgroup began design of DITA in late 1999 and worked on it during 2000.

The goal of the workgroup was to design an architecture for information interchange, provide the tools to do so, and have the system be extensible. The decision was made to build the architecture on top of XML because XML was a leading technology at the time and was able to be produced and consumed by a wide variety of communities of data owners.

Many companies like IBM have very diverse delivery systems (such as print, web pages, PDF, etc.), which need to be tied together. While it is futile to attempt providing one common tool for all delivery systems, having one common data exchange format that is standards based is more practical.

The IBM workgroup also did not want to craft an architecture that only worked for legacy practices, but one that was fully extensible so that it can be of use even when needs and systems change in the future. That lead the workgroup members to the awareness that the issues in front of them could not be simply translated into DTDs. There was another aspect to consider, and that was how the entire process from authoring to delivering worked and how technical information is designed. This lead to the borrowing of approaches such that are used in HTML. For example, ordered or unordered lists can be copied from HTML without any need for modification. This process lead to the Darwin Information Typing Architecture (DITA), which was adapted as an international standard by the Organization for the Advancement of Structured Information Standards (OASIS) in June 2005. DITA is named after Charles Darwin.

Topic orientation

Topics are the highest standard structure in DITA and have no internal hierarchical nesting. Topics are the building blocks that are used during output processing when, for example, the navigation for online help is added. Topics are used for different needs and generally three types of topics are found in most documentation: concept, reference, and task or procedure. DITA already has these three basic topic classes defined, but can be expanded to manage more topic classes when needed. See section 4.3 "Topic Classes".

Reuse

DITA has two types of organized reuse. One is the reuse of topics. Since the topics itself are not further nested they can be used in any context where they fit. The second type of reuse is content reuse. Each content element has a reference that can be used within the same topic or any other topic. The referenced element replaces a base element in the topic to make sure that even when the reference cannot be found the structure stays intact.

Specialization

DITA has several base elements that can be modified through attributes. It is also possible to define new attributes so that new elements and new topic types can be crafted. This allows adjusting DITA to work for various contexts that have special requirements for the documentation process. Therefore, this process is called specialization. Committees of OASIS crafted industry specific specializations that were standardized, such as for the semiconductor industry, the machine industry, learning and training applications, and enterprise business documentation.

Property-based processing

The DITA model provides extensive metadata and universal properties. The metadata can be used for filtering and searching content, which makes topics easier to find. The properties are designed in such a way that they allow for a wide range of enumerated values so that they can be used for diverse types of specializations that typically restrict values rather than adding new ones.

Taking advantage of existing tags and tools

DITA was not supposed to reinvent the wheel. Tags and tools that were proven to work well and that fit the DITA model were implemented into the architecture. For example the P, OL, and UL tags from XHTML are used in DITA without modification. This makes it easier to build rendering engines that can display DITA content in a browser. Since DITA is XML based, any XML tools can be used to create, modify, and process DITA files. This also allows for combining DITA with Cascading Style Sheets (CSS), Extensible Stylesheet Language Transformations (XSLT), and also Extensible Stylesheet Language Formatting Objects (XSL-FO). This way DITA document sets can be converted into web pages, PDF, HTMLHelp, Eclipse Help, Java Help, Oracle Help, and Rich Text Format. A set of tools to preform these conversions is available through DITA Open Toolkit (DITA OT), which is provided by IBM. The kit contains free and open-source tools such as converters, editors, and stylesheets. There are also plenty of other tools available outside of DITA OT. For example, DITA debugging tools written in PHP.

4.3 Topic Classes

Topics are the core of any help. One can approach the term topic from various angles:

- For a reader the topic is the information that is displayed in the help window.

- Technically speaking, a topic is a (HTML/XML) file or part of a (Word) file.

- In regards to content logic, a topic is a complete self-contained information unit.

Topics should be small enough to allow flexible use, but they also should not be too small so that there is no decrease in efficiency for both author and reader. A topic should be a self-contained, general information unit. General is meant in regards to other topics, but not the graphical user interface. A possible context is created through links to other topics.

Division into classes means assigning topics based on their content to categories through use of specific criteria. A topic class is a collection of topics of the same kind. For example topics can be classified based on the content being a description or an instruction. This generally matches the information classes in information design or the sequence patterns in function design.

Over time, the following information or topic classes developed and are listed in the Microsoft style guide as:

- concept
- reference
- procedure
- context sensitive help at the dialog box and element level
- glossary

Looking at the classes a bit closer shows that "concept" and "reference" are part of the superclass "description" and are therefore a subclass. The context sensitive topics can be ascribed to references. "Procedure" is only a different name for "instruction". DITA also has similar topic classes.

4.3.1 Concept Topics

Concept topics contain introductory and overview information, such as function overviews, process descriptions, or change and release notes. Concept topics contain background information that is necessary for understanding the procedures.

4.3.2 Reference Topics

Reference topics are like online encyclopedias. They describe not only the graphical user interface, but also parts of a programming language or interface. The purpose of a reference topic determines the use of text and pictures.

4.3.3 Procedure Topics

A procedure topic contains the steps that are necessary to accomplish a task or reach a goal. Procedure topics should only contain the necessary steps. They are not intended to provide information about the task.

Procedures should use a consistent scheme. The sequence of the individual steps is based on the chronological sequence. Each step should describe the feedback provided by the product if applicable, for example the opening of a dialog box or a message.

Additional information, alternative approaches, or related topics are accessible for the reader through links and link bundles (see chapter 6 "Navigation").

4.3.4 Glossary Topics

A simple example for a glossary topic is the explanation of a technical term. When the explanation of a technical term is organized as an individual topic it can be referenced in all those places where the technical term is used.

4.3.5 DITA Topic Classes and Maps

The DITA model has three basic topic classes: concept, reference, and task or procedure. These topic classes are described in the previous sections of this book. DITA allows for crafting additional topic classes, such as tutorial or glossary topics. The main topic classes themselves can be specialized as well. For example, complicated tasks require a different topic class than small, simple tasks. In that case it may be beneficial to create the topic class "minitask". In the same way other topic classes can be specialized. The topics each have a reference.

The various topics that are each associated with a class are not independent pieces of information. A task relates to a concept which relates to a reference, which itself also relates to the concept and the task. These relationships are defined in relationship tables (see section 6.6.6.4 "Relationship Tables").

The DITA model also allows for referencing external objects, which can be DITA or non-DITA objects. These references and hierarchies are combined into a DITA map. A maps also has a reference and thus can be referenced by other maps.

4.4   Conclusion for Online Help

An online help system is supposed to support the user while working with a product (for example software). The help system is supposed to offer users the information that is needed to accomplish the tasks quickly and reliably.

Although it is often different in practice, an online help system is not a replacement for a manual. Ideally, an online help system complements a manual by providing descriptions of the graphical user interface and step-by-step instructions so that the information provided by both media overlaps meaningfully.

4.4.1   Determining the Document Structure

The first step for a topic breakdown is the analysis of the information and making a decision on how the information is to be created and managed. There are two different approaches for this:

- For the information in an online help system and a book, various sources and tools are used which are optimized for the specific medium.

- All information is collected in one topic-oriented source. After the collection process is completed a decision is made on which information is used for online help system or for a book. This approach is more flexible and called Single Sourcing.

Both approaches eventually require a decision regarding which information the readers will receive from the book or the online help.

4.4.1.1 *Information for Online Help*

The following pieces of information need to be in an online help:

- Reference to the corresponding product (identification) so that the user knows that he or she is working with the correct online help (ideally, the identification is in the title bar of the help system).

- Safety information when the product can cause bodily harm or loss of life, or when loss of data is possible as far as it relates to the information in the help. This information can be provided in its own chapter or at the place where the danger can occur.

- An introduction as an orientation for users with the following information about:

  - purpose of the online help and its parts

  - intended use of the product

  - target group(s) of the online help or its parts

  - graphical elements used in the help (such as notification symbols, etc.)

  - purpose of the product

  - short overview of the product features

  - product changes from previous versions

- Description of all user interface elements (such as menus, commands, buttons) that the user can directly see and access.

- A description in sufficient detail of all messages in regards to known problems that can occur during use of the product.

- Sufficient navigation such as a table of contents or an index, so that the user can find the provided information in the online help.

- Help for using the online help system unless this is provided from the operating system (such as Windows), or when the individual functions differ from the standard.

- Process instructions that support the user while working with the product. These instructions are problem and task oriented.

- Solutions to the most common problems and description of the problem sources (FAQ).

Due to resource limits not all information can be included in online help. The last two points of this list can be seen as optional, but the first six items are minimum requirements for a user-friendly online help.

4.4.1.2 Information for Books

Businesses often do not print manuals (hand books) for cost reasons. All information has to be included in the online help without regards to whether it is useful or not. This is why some online help systems include content that is not mentioned in the list above. This information is typically better presented in a book because it goes beyond the purpose of online help, which is providing punctual support. Some examples are:

- Concept information necessary for the use of the product. It is intended to provide a basic context and is supposed to enhance the user's understanding of the product, so that the user can use special features or comprehend erroneous behavior. Concept information is not intended for solving specific problems, but to provide knowledge about the design of the product. Examples for concept information are:

  ■ functional principle of the product

- concepts and principles of the product

- process overview (text, graphics)

- strategies for the use of the product (efficient ways for using the product)

- visible product structure

- internal logic of the product (hidden functional dependencies, such as distributed parameters)

- general explanations for error conditions

- sources and literature links

- References that include all information about the software or product, which are not included in the user interface documentation (such as command line commands, instructions or parameters of a programming language, etc). This information is often organized like a reference book so that the user can quickly and directly access information about the program. User interface documentation and reference information can complement each other. The program description is more helpful as a printed reference book.

4.4.1.3   *Information for Paper*

There is information that needs to be provided through a different medium, which is typically paper. Product liability laws may require that safety information is printed on paper if the product may cause harm or death. Furthermore, information on paper needs to be provided if otherwise the user would receive this information too late. For example, system prerequisites, technical data, or installation instructions that are not context sensitive.

4.4.2   Determining Topic Classes

Topic classes can be determined once it is decided how the information is created and organized. Two main classes are already established:

- instructions

- descriptions

Both main classes can be broken down further to suit the requirements of the products. For example, a product can be operated by simple tasks and have processes that are compiled from these tasks. The description class can be split into:

- introduction / overview

- dialog box description

- element descriptions (for dialog boxes)

- user interface descriptions (menus, commands, icons, etc)

- additional classes

Each topic class has characteristics and structure defined. Typical characteristics are:

- class name

- naming convention for file name

- access options

- allowed links

4.4.3   Determining the Structure of a Topic Class

The structure of a topic class determines which types of information (information mapping) or which functional units (functional design) are allowed in that topic class. It is recommended to create a template for each topic class that shows the allowed and optional units. For the topic class "Task" the template might look like this:

> **Title (Goal description)**
> Short description of the task (without links)
> **[Prerequisites]**
> **[Warnings]**
> **Steps**
> 1. Step without links
> 2. ...
> 3. ...
> **[Result]**
> ***
> **Further Information**
> Concept link
> **Related Tasks**
> Link to task

Figure 22: Template for topic class "task"

The tags and styles for each element can now be defined with the help of the template. For example, some titles such as "Prerequisites" and "Result" always have to appear as such. One can develop exact style guides for each topic class. For example, a rule for titles is created to always place the verb at the end for a task description (example: "File saving") or use a noun for a user interface description (example: "Menu File").

DITA has by default three topic classes: concept, reference, and task or procedure. Each topic class should be structured based on the type of information or the functional unit. These basic topic classes can be expanded by additional topic classes if needed. See section 4.3.5 "DITA Topic Classes and Maps".

4.5 Implementation with Flare

Most of the contents of this chapter impact a Flare project only indirectly so that only general tasks such as "Creating a Topic" or "Editing a Topic" are covered. When working with topic classes one can create a template for each topic class. See section 4.5.5 "Templates".

4.5.1 Creating a Topic

To create a topic do the following:

1. Select the **Content Explorer**.

2. Select the folder in the **Content Explorer** in which the new topic is to be added.

3. Select the command **Project > Add Topic**. The dialog box **Add New Topic** appears.

4. Select a different **Template** for the new topic if desired, see section 4.5.5 "Templates".

5. Check if **Folder** specifies to the desired folder, otherwise select a different one.

6. Enter a **File Name** for the new topic.

7. If desired, select the **1ˢᵗ Heading** and assign a suitable **Style**.

8. Verify that the correct stylesheet is selected in **Stylesheet**, otherwise select a different one.

9. Accept the settings by clicking on **Add**. The dialog box closes and a confirmation message appears indicating that the new topic file is copied to the specified destination.

10. Proceed by clicking on **OK**. The dialog box closes, the new topic is added to the selected folder, and the topic is opened in the XML editor for editing. When no folder was selected the new topic is placed in the folder **Content**.

4.5.2 Importing a Topic

Flare allows importing existing topics from other projects or HTML files. For importing a topic do the following:

1. Select the **Content Explorer**.

2. Select the folder in the **Content Explorer** in which the new topic is to be added.

3. Select the command **Project > Add Topic**. The dialog box **Add New Topic** appears.

4. Click on the **...** (ellipsis) button of **Source File** and select the file to import using the **Open** dialog box.

5. Verify if the entry in **Folder** is the correct folder for the topic file to be copied into, otherwise select a different folder.

6. If desired give the topic a new **File Name**.

7. Select the desired option in **Stylesheet**.

8. Accept the settings by clicking on **Add**. The dialog box closes and a confirmation message appears indicating that the new topic file is copied to the specified destination.

9. Confirm by clicking **OK**. The dialog box closes and

   - the topic is copied into the specified folder and opened in the XML editor for editing. The topic will be copied to the folder **Content** when no folder was specified.

   - when the topic to be imported is not an XML file a confirmation message appears asking if the file should be converted to XML. The file can be converted immediately or at a later point. When selecting to have the file converted at a later point it will be converted to XML the first time it is opened.

4.5.3   Topic Properties

The properties of a topic can be changed in the **Properties** dialog box. The **Properties** dialog box is opened as follows:

1. Open the **Content Explorer**.

2. Right-click on the desired topic and select **Properties** from the context menu. The dialog box **Properties** opens.

The properties of a topic are organized in

Basic   General file properties

Topic Properties   Special topic properties

Conditional Text   Possible conditions for the topic

Snippet Conditions Possible conditions for the topic when it is used as a snippet

Language   Language used in the topic

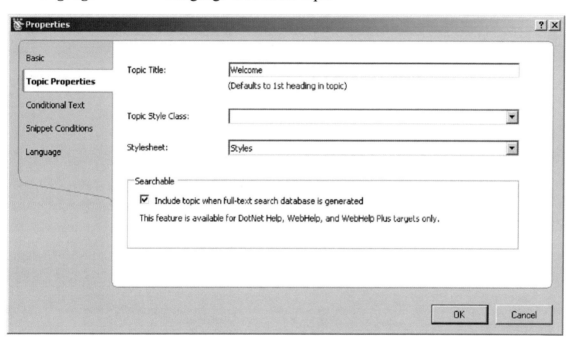

Figure 23: Properties of a topic

The property **Topic Title** has a special function. It is not necessarily the heading of the topic text, but it is its own element, which is used for various features:

- topic name in the table of contents, see section 6.6.1 "Table of Contents"

- topic name used in the breadcrumbs proxy, see section 5.7.1 "Master Pages"

- topic name in the menu that appears when multiple hits were found in the index, see section 6.6.2 "Index"

- topic name in the menu shown in the "See Also" links, see section 6.6.6 ""See Also" Links"

- topic name in the menu that appears when multiple hits were found in a full text search

Flare automatically generates a topic title from the heading of the text for both imported and newly added topics. It is possible to change the entry in **Topic Title** to be different than the heading. For example, when the text used for breadcrumbs needs to be shorter. It is recommended to keep heading and topic title the same to give the reader a better orientation.

4.5.4 Editing a Topic

A topic can be edited in the XML editor the same way as in any other editor by placing the cursor at the desired position and entering text. The text is formatted by using the symbols in the text format toolbar or through the style window (see section "Assign individual styles" in section 5.7.2 "Stylesheets"). The following sections describe working with:

- lists

- tables

- templates

4.5.4.1 *Lists*

Flare offers ordered and unordered lists. Flare offers the following bullets:

- bullet point
- circle
■ square
123 arabic numbers
abc lower case letters

ABC   upper case letters

iii   lower case roman numerals

III   upper case roman numerals

Inserting a list

1. Select the **Content Explorer**.

2. Double-click on the topic in which the list is supposed to get inserted.

3. Select the paragraphs that are to be converted into a list.

4. Choose the command **Format > List** and choose the desired list format. The paragraphs will be formatted using the selected list format.

Editing a list

The structure of the XML file can be viewed in the XML editor using the following icons in the toolbar at the bottom of the XML editor:

Toggles the XML block tags left of the topic on or off.

Toggles the XML span and div tags at the top of the topic on or off.

The entire list can be easily edited using the displayed XML tags:

1. Toggle the XML block tags left of the topic on.

2. Click with the right mouse button in the XML structure bar on the list tags (OL or UL).

3. Choose the desired command from the context menu (**Sort List, Reverse List, Unbind List**)

It is further possible to edit the individual list elements using the displayed XML tags:

1. Click with the right mouse button in the XML structure bar on a list element tag (LI).

2. Choose the desired command from the context menu (**Move Up**, **Move Down**, **Move Left**).

4.5.4.2   Tables

Tables can be formatted by creating individual table styles that are assigned to tables. Table styles are stored in the **Content Explorer** as table stylesheets in the folder **Resources / Stylesheets**.

Inserting a Table

1. Select the **Content Explorer**.

2. Double-click on the topic in which the table needs to be inserted.

3. Place the cursor at the position where the table is supposed to be inserted.

4. Select the command **Table > Insert > Table**. The dialog box **Insert Table** appears.

5. Enter the **Number of columns** on the **Basic** tab.

6. Enter the **Number of rows**.

7. Enter the **Number of header rows** and **Number of footer rows** if desired.

8. Specify the width of the table in **AutoFit Behavior**:

AutoFit to contents	The columns are adjusted based on their contents.
AutoFit to window	The column widths are evenly distributed based on the selected amount of the window width.
Fixed column width	Each column has a fixed width.

9. Select the table alignment in **Align**.

10. Choose the desired border settings for the table on the **Border** tab.

11. Click **OK** to accept the settings. The dialog box closes and the table is inserted into the topic.

Editing a table

The table structure can be displayed by clicking on the following icons in the local toolbar at the bottom of the topic.

Toggles the table row bars on and off.

Toggles the table column bars on and off.

The entire table can be comfortably edited using the structure bars:

1. Toggle the table structure bars on.

2. Right-click on a structure bar for a column or row. A context menu opens for the selected element. From there one can

   - change the column width

   - change the row height

   - insert a new row or column

   - delete the contents of the row or column

The structure bars also allow moving rows or columns.

1. Hover the mouse pointer over the structure bar of the row or column to be moved until the pointer shows a small rectangle: .

2. Hold down the left mouse button and move the table element until a blue arrow appears.

3. Release the mouse button and the table element is moved to the position of the blue arrow.

Creating a table style

1. Select the command **Project > Add Table Style**. The dialog box **Add New Table Style** opens.

2. Select a **Template**, for example for a row style.

3. Enter a **File Name**.

4. Accept the settings with **Add** and the dialog box closes. The dialog box **Copy to Project** opens, click **OK** to close this dialog box and proceed. The table style is created in the folder **Resources / TableStyles** and opened for editing.

5. The following settings are available from the **General** tab:

   - Outer Borders

   - Cell Padding

   - Table Margins

   - Cell Border Collapse

   - Cell Border Spacing

6. The tabs **Rows**, **Columns**, **Header**, and **Footer** allow for setting a pattern:

   - The list **Pattern** shows the defined patterns and the repetition rate. By default, two patterns exist that alternate the background color of the table rows. New patterns can be added, or the existing ones can be edited or deleted.

   - The **Pattern Properties** allow editing the selected pattern, for example the repetition rate and the background color can be set.

7. Save the table style with the command **File > Save**.

Assigning a table style

1. Place the cursor into the table which needs to have a table format assigned.

2. Select the command **Table > Table Properties**. The dialog box **Table Properties** opens.

3. Select the **Basic** tab and choose from the list **Table Style** the style to be assigned to the table.

4. Accept the settings by clicking on **OK**. The dialog box closes and the table style is assigned to the table.

4.5.5 Templates

Flare uses a template for every element, no matter if it is a topic or a control file. Flare comes with a default set of templates for each element beginning with the Flare project itself. When adding a new element such as a topic or a stylesheet one has to select a template first, which is then copied into the project.

Templates help in keeping consistency across all projects for a company or a customer. It is possible to create a template for each topic class. This provides consistency across the project, especially when multiple writers work on one project.

Templates can also save work because a template can be created for each topic or control file. This allows important settings for a target definition or a skin to be set once and then used over and over again. First create a folder called "My Templates" in the folder `C:\Documents and Settings\<user name>\My Documents\`. Then create a folder structure based on the type of template file using the table below as a reference. Only when the template files are in the correctly named folder in the My Templates folder will Flare be able to pick them up and offer them as selections.

Table 8: Folder names for templates

File	Folder name	File	Folder name
Alias file	Advanced	Search Filter Set	Advanced
Browse Sequences	Advanced	Skin	Skins
Conditional Tags Set	ConditionalTagSets	Snippet	Snippets
Destination	Destinations	Stylesheet	Stylesheets
FrameMake Import	Imports	Synonym file	Advanced
Glossary	Glossaries	Table of contents	TOCs

File	Folder name
Header file	Advanced
Master page	MasterPages
MS Word Import	Imports
Pictures	Images
Project	Projects

File	Folder name
Table Style	TableStyles
Target definition	Targets
Topic	Content
Variable Set	VariableSets

For example, once templates for new topics are placed into the **Content** folder under **My Templates** the templates show in **Templates** when selecting **My Templates** in the list **Template Folders**.

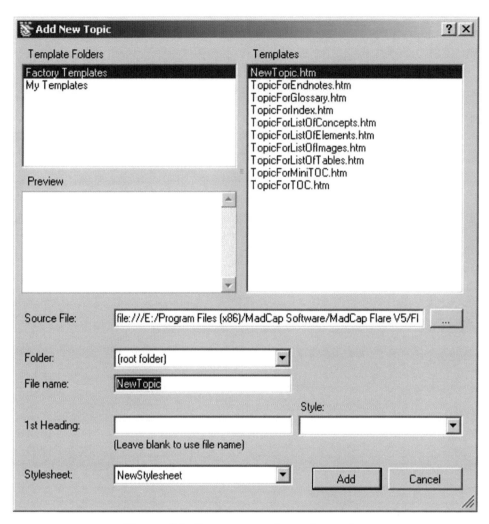

Figure 24: Custom templates for topics

5 Layout

Reading on screen is more cumbersome than reading on paper. Various studies until the 1990s show that readers of text on paper can read faster, longer, and also retain more of the content read compared to readers of text on screen. The speed of reading also depends on the monitor settings, which often provide a lower resolution compared to paper. Newer studies show that the reading speed is about the same compared to paper when using flicker-free, high resolution monitors.

The layout of online help is intended to support the comprehensibility of text and with that support the readability and legibility. The legibility of a text is determined by how fast it can be read, while readability refers to how easy a text can be read, understood, and comprehended. The legibility refers to the styling of the characters, lines, and areas of a text, while the readability refers to the choice of words and language. The layout is supposed to support the presentation of the contents to the human receptiveness ("Don't make me think").

Reading

Readable texts support the reading process, the medium (screen or paper), and the reader's expectations of gain. During reading the eyes follow the written lines from left to right. Word silhouettes are recognized and the impulses are transferred to the brain.

The recognized words are compared to words already stored in memory and then deciphered. This takes more time for long or compounded words, because the eyes can only focus on a few millimeters. Reading long words requires capturing these millimeter steps, compiling them in short term memory, and then comparing them to the terms stored in memory: searching for meaning. New words are interpreted through context and then classified.

The more words a person knows, the faster and more fluent one can read. The readability is dependent on the choice of words, and the comprehension is dependent on the context. Language or text structure and text organization respectively control the readability and user friendliness of online help.

Reading is a learned process. Since centuries we are trained by the occidental culture to read from left to right and top to bottom. Orientation from paragraph to paragraph and fluent reading from line to line are the basis of any text organization.

Searching

An online help has to support various search strategies. Depending on the screen used the reading can be 33% slower compared to reading the same text from paper. The reader does not read accurately, but performs "scanning" as Jacob Nielsen calls it. This means that during the search for relevant information the eyes jump from alert to alert, always on the search for anchor words, which are expected to lead to the desired information.

Cognitive psychology defines scanning in a similar way and differentiates between two types of attention: hovering and focused attention. Users with hovering attention have an unclear view of the entire content and scan the text based on portions that stand out. These users capture a broad amount of information in parallel, which is about 50% of the entire topic.

A user with focused attention captures only the currently suitable information. Anything distracting is ignored or filtered out as much as possible, the user skims the topic. The processing capacity is lower compared to the hovering attention and only about 30% of the entire content of a topic is captured. A varied presentation is best suited for the first type of reader, while it frustrates the second type of reader. The second type requires a good index or a full text search.

Users expect to find the same type of information in always the same place. Consistency is the most important criterion for fulfilling this expectation and for creating a well made layout. A constant reorientation does not provide for good readability.

Many scientists researched the specifics of reading and understanding of text on screen and also looked at supporting layouts. Especially in the beginnings of the World Wide Web many usability tests were performed whose results can be applied to online help. These tests showed that readers are very easily distracted by too many elements on a page.

5.1 Page Layout

The criterion for designing online help is the output medium: the computer monitor. Its strengths and weaknesses in displaying determine the styling of text and graphics. In comparison to paper, computer monitors have a fixed size and a lower resolution as well as lower contrast. Since monitors are typically wider than they are high it makes more sense to use landscape than the portrait format, which is common for paper.

The suitable amount of information for a help page is not only determined by the page format, but also how the user will make use of the help. Usability tests showed that users focus on the center of the screen and often do not realize that additional information is in a currently invisible area that needs to be scrolled to. The same applies to information in the upper section of the screen. These contents are recognized only after the third or fourth time the page was requested.

Two opinions exist about how much information is to be placed on a help page: should contents that belong together be placed on different pages (paging) or should all contents be of one long page (scrolling). Jacob Nielson found out from usability tests that users do not like to click for scrolling and would rather see all information in one view. In contrast, Jared Spool showed that users are absolutely willing to scroll through a longer page when they are convinced that they can find additional relevant information.

The conclusion can only be to combine both approaches and present information as compact as possible so that only a few clicks are necessary to access all content.

Usability experts define the following demands for page layouts:

- flexible layout that adjusts to the screen and browser window width of the user's system
- no horizontal paging

- short pages

- important information needs to be accessible without paging or scrolling ("above the fold")

5.2   Font

Unlike on paper, small serif fonts are more difficult to read on screen than non-serif fonts. This is caused by screen resolution: the average resolution of 72 dpi produces a pixel size of about 0.35 mm, which is similar to the size of a typographic dot. Basically, this results to: the smaller the screen font is, the finer the lines are and the more difficult it is to display them on screen.

Serif-accented fonts with wide flowing characters are easy to read, for example, Courier. Text on screen should use a bigger font scale compared to paper for ergonomic reasons because the reading distance is larger.

The tracking (distance between characters) of some fonts is too narrow for use on screen. It appears as if the characters touch each other or flow together and that causes an "r" and an "n" to appear as an "m". This makes reading more difficult. One remedy is spacing. This correction is direly necessary when using bright text on a colored or black background because the blooming reduces the space between characters on screen optically.

Fonts exist that were specially designed for reading on screen, such as Tahoma, Geneva, Verdana, or Chicago. Their typeface is adjusted to the 72 dpi screen resolution. The readability of a font also depends on the font scale, which has to be coordinated with the page layout and the anticipated screen size and screen resolution.

Suitable word spacing defines clear word silhouettes. Spacing that is too small disturbs the flow of reading and thus interferes with text comprehension. Too large or irregular word spacing is user-unfriendly because it disturbs the flow of reading as well. This is often caused by improper justification: a character amount per line that is too low or a "forced" justification.

Line spacing that is too small disturbs the flow of reading. The word silhouettes are disturbed by the lower line following too closely and it is more difficult to find the beginning of the next line. Indention, when the beginning of the first line of a paragraph is moved to the right. can help with orientation in longer texts. Short lines with a maximum of 55 to 60 characters are easier to understand when read on screen.

Text markups further guide the eyes during scanning of a page. It is very common to use bold font for user interface elements. As common, is underlining of links. The use of such de-facto standards makes using the help system easier because the user has to learn fewer new concepts and can use existing knowledge.

Italics should be used sparingly, because they appear distorted and fuzzy. Also, using majuscules (capital letters) for headings or for text markup is not a good choice. Majuscules disable the original word silhouette and make scanning the text more difficult. The same applies to double markups. The screen requires its own layout rules, but that does not mean that all other rules for good layouts are no longer valid.

5.3 Language

A lot has been written and researched about text comprehensibility and language. To summarize, it has been determined that using common words, known terminology, and accurate verbs in short, straightforward sentences make texts easier to read and easier to understand. The better an author matches the language of the target group the higher the acceptance of the text read. The clearer statements are the better the chance content will be understood and remembered.

Headings should summarize the content that follows and not be a play on words or be ironic. The most important information should be placed at the beginning of the text. Scanning is made easier when each page starts with a different word and generally the text has a distinctive structure. One of the biggest demands for creating comprehensible text is concise formulation.

Furthermore, text should not be written in marketing jargon, which contains little or no useful information and does not satisfy the expectations of the users.

5.4 Colors

Colors not only get the reader's attention, but they also create emotions and convey messages. Human color reception is based on various aspects. Biologically speaking, various colors are assessed differently because there are a different number of photo receptors in the human eye. Sixty-four percent of the photo receptors are for red, but only two percent are for blue. Color blindness is also caused by biological aspects, such as the common red-green blindness. Colors are also influenced by cultural aspects and colors can have varying meanings in different cultures. For example, some cultures connect black to sadness, but in other cultures it is white.

Psychological aspects also play a role in perception. Color psychology asserts that colors trigger associations and emotions that are based on individual experiences. Additionally, "archetypical associations", which are cultural knowledge or unconscious collective awareness, influence the color sensation.

Colors are also attributed to symbolic powers. For example, blue symbolizes heaven and eternity, and yellow symbolizes time and transience. Lastly, personal preferences, experiences, and trends influence the individual color reception.

Nevertheless, color can improve the transport of information when used consistently, for example the color red as support (signal color) for warnings. Colors can also be used as styles for foreground to background relationships, distinctions, or be used in symbols.

There are eight base colors: the achromatic base colors black and white and the six chromatic base colors red, yellow, green, cyan, blue, and magenta. The display on screen works through the additive color system, the RGB model, named after the initial letters of the three base colors red, green, and blue. All three together produce white. When two base colors overlap a new color is created, the so called secondary color: red and green produce yellow, red and blue make magenta (purple), and blue and green result in cyan (cyan blue).

Colors on screen are put together differently than pigmented colors on paper. On paper the CMYK model is used: the pigmented colors of four color printing are cyan blue, magenta red, yellow, and key (black, contrast). On a white background they reflect the residual light, printed together they give black. Screen displays are never the same as the print results because prints on paper are only possible using the CMYK model.

The special characteristics of screen displays need to be considered when choosing colors for online help. The screen is an active light source, so blooming can occur. Reading for a long period of time tires out the eyes and is not comfortable. This can be compensated for by using a light colored background, for example, light gray or yellow. Newer studies show that we see black font on white background as having the most contrast, which means it can be read the easiest.

When selecting colors for online help the following criteria also have to play a role besides the corporate design rules, which exist in many companies as style guides:

- recognition of the appearance
- good readability of texts and images
- navigation and user guidance through the systematic use of colors
- contrast

Although there are no general guidelines for the use of colors, one should follow the old typographic rule of "less is more" when working with colors and other styles.

5.5 Pictures

Pictures in online help can fulfill various functions in the learning and memorization process and convey contents not only linguistically, but also visually. Pictures are beneficial when they contain relevant information and are related to the text information.

Results of imagery research show that pictures are received and processed without much thought effort. They are also easily recognized and have a strong emotional influence. Combinations of text and pictures can greatly improve recognition.

Abstract terms and logical relationships are often difficult to describe with visual analogies or symbols. Logical links between statements (although, notwithstanding, if / then) and negations are also difficult to visualize. Simplified pictures can be ambiguous and convey unintentional messages.

Descriptive text is needed to reduce the ambiguity of a picture and limit the possible interpretations for a reader. Text and picture have to relate to and complement each other in order to generate an integrated total comprehension. Three types of text-picture relationships in regards to content are differentiated:

- congruent relationship: the text describes what the picture shows
- complementary relationship: the picture supplements the text (and vice versa); analysis of both components is necessary for total comprehension
- elaborative relationship: the text goes beyond the contents of the picture (and vice versa); an elaborative relationship is only useful when the necessary knowledge can be assumed to be present

Close spatial proximity is a precondition for the collaboration of text and pictures. Linguistic cues are picture headings, picture captions, or a picture key. Visual cues are, for example, arrows and colored accentuations. Linguistic references between text and picture should match. In general, two types of pictures are differentiated: static and dynamic pictures.

5.5.1 Static Pictures

Static pictures are pictures without any form of movement, animation, or interaction. The two types of static pictures are realistic and abstract images:

- realistic images deliver an almost realistic picture of real figures. Among these are photos, line drawings, schema drawings, exploded views, and screen shots, which are reproductions of parts of the graphical user interface. They are replacements for reality and represent visual knowledge about the appearance of items and spatial relationships.

- abstract images are also called instructional pictures. They clarify logical relationships and examples are diagrams, models, or tables. Icons are also part of this category.

A simplified display focuses on the relevant picture content and reduces distraction. A simplification of pictures includes the following steps:

- removal of irrelevant content

- emphasis of important content

- grouping of related contents

Spatial organization is especially important for processing. A reasonable arrangement makes it easier for the user to get oriented and be able to memorize the picture as part of a meaningful general context.

Screen shots are not recommended for context sensitive help. This is also recommended by the standard ISO/IEC 18019 "Software and system engineering – Guidelines for the design and preparation of user documentation for application software".

The user can "get lost" in the windows, which means the user clicks on a symbol in the screen shot in the online help and wonders why nothing happens. When there is a dire need for the technical writer to present screen shots for the sake of better understanding then the screen shot should be rendered as such by showing only a section or torn edges.

5.5.2 Dynamic Pictures

Dynamic pictures are, for example, videos or animations and are especially suited for displaying movements, trajectories, changes, and chronological sequences. A special type of dynamic picture is an interactive picture (simulation). A dynamic picture can make an item more attractive. The visualization can facilitate the understanding and support memorization.

All types of visualization strive to transform information into a meaningful and usable display, which allows the reader to analyze the basic information. Some information is more easily conveyed using dynamic pictures than static pictures:

- transitions: visualization of different status changes of a system (for example, instantly or gradually)
- sequences: visualization of time based phenomena
- multiple coding: visualization of multiple information in the same location (for example, through mouse-over effects)
- activities: visualization of uncommon tasks

The diversity of dynamic displays includes the danger of sensory overload. That is why information that is conveyed through picture and sound has to be carefully tuned. Purposefully used multimedia in online help can have a positively motivating effect. The technical possibilities for creating multimedia can lead to overloading media with too many dynamic elements and produce a feeling of being rushed. An overloaded online help distracts from the underlying content.

Usability experts demand the following from dynamic pictures:

- that the user is informed about size and format of the media file,

- that the user can control the replay of continuous media files,

- that the user can mute the sound,

- and that there are no infinite loops.

5.5.3 Graphic Formats

Only a few specific graphic formats are suitable for screen display, such as bitmaps for icons and symbols, or GIF/JPEG pictures. Lossless and lossy compression processes such as JPEG reduce the file size and thus speed up the display on screen. The same speed enhancement have interlaced GIF images that are drawn line by line on screen.

5.6 Conclusion for Online Help

Online help works well with a simple layout. The almost standardized help window determines some areas for which the technical writer does not have to make intensive efforts: the navigation on the left side of the help window and the toolbar.

The technical writer can select the content of the navigation and toolbar and choose how the content is to be displayed. For example, having a two-level index in the navigation or a print button in the toolbar to print the currently displayed text. This means that the design of an online help focuses on the text layout and text amount.

Font and Text Structure

It is recommended that a sans-serif font that is optimized for display on screen be used, such as Verdana. This font should also be available on most computer systems because web browsers can only display those fonts that are installed on the client system. The browser will use its default font when the specified font is not available (typically Times New Roman for Windows and Times for Mac OS). This problem can be solved by embedding the specific font file.

Structural elements such as headings, enumerations, lists, and tables support the scanning of information. The headings should stand out from the regular text and include sufficient white space. White space itself is also a structural element.

Colors and Screen Resolution

Colors capture the viewer's attention and can be used for information. In online help colors are usually used for links. This requires two colors, one for the link itself and a weaker color for a visited link. Analyzing the corporate identity of the customer requesting the online help can aid in selecting the colors. It is acceptable to use the de-facto standard blue if the analysis does not provide any suitable color choice.

Jacob Nielsen recommends a screen resolution of 1024x768 for optimized display of the help window. Currently, 60% of all monitors are set to a resolution of 1024x768. In comparison, only 17% of all users still use a resolution of 800x600. An adjustable layout is recommended since the majority share is likely to shift due to the advent of monitors with higher resolutions.

5.7 Implementation with Flare

The layout for online help is controlled in Flare through master pages, stylesheets, and the skin. It is possible to embed pictures, movies, and sound in topics.

5.7.1 Master Pages

A master page determines the general look of a help page. For example, it is possible to add a header, footer, or a company logo. A master page has to be assigned to help pages. The effects of a master page can only be seen after generating the help. A project can make use of multiple master pages, for example, for various clients or different products that are covered within one project.

For print-based outputs the use of page layouts is recommended over the user of master pages. Page layouts allow for easy configuration of content frames, left and right pages, and other more print specific layout settings.

Proxies

Proxies are small programs that have been especially developed for use with master pages. Proxies generate on each help page specific entries that were defined by the master page. The best example is the body proxy, which represents the main content of a help page. At compile time the content of the topic is inserted at the location of the body proxy. The body proxy also determines header and footer. Anything above the body proxy is considered a header and anything below is a footer. The following table lists some proxies that are especially created for online help. The position of these proxies can be changed on the master page or they can also be deleted.

Table 9: Proxy types in Flare

Proxy type	Explanation
Breadcrumbs proxy	The breadcrumbs proxy displays one row in the first line of the help page. The navigation path is generated at compile time and is based on the links in the table of contents. It is important to link the books in the table of contents as well so that each element of the breadcrumbs resolves to a link to a topic. The breadcrumbs proxy is recommended to be at the top of a help page because it supports the orientation within the help. The one -line display saves space.
Mini-ToC proxy	The mini-ToC proxy produces a small table of contents typically at the bottom of a help page. The mini-ToC proxy feeds off the main table of contents. The mini-ToC proxy is not very common in practice because it uses a lot of space and is often not seen since it is at the bottom of a page.
Relationships proxy	The relationships proxy is based on the entries in the corresponding relationship tables. Based on which entries were populated in the relationship table and how the link types were set, the relationships proxy is replaced with sections for "Related Information", "Related Tasks", or "Reference Material" respectively. Although relationship tables and therefore relationships proxies are typically associated with DITA document sets, both can be used with any type of output Flare can generate.
Topic toolbar proxy	The topic toolbar proxy allows placing an additional toolbar anywhere inside a topic. The topic toolbar proxy can be added to individual topics as well as to a master page. The contents of the topic toolbar are specified by settings that can be edited from the Skin Editor and also at the time the proxy is added. Available toolbar buttons are, for example, "Next Topic", "Previous Topic", "Back", "Home", "Print", or "Quick Search".

Creating a Master Page

To create a new master page follow these steps:

1. Select the command **Project** > **Add Master Page...** . The dialog box **Add New Master Page** opens.

2. Select a template for the new master page from **Templates**. Flare offers the template MasterPage.flmsp for online help. All other templates are for printed output.

3. Enter a name for the master page into **File Name**.

4. Verify that the desired stylesheet is specified in the **Stylesheet** selection.

5. Click on **Add** to create the new master page. The dialog box closes and a new dialog box **Copy to Project** opens asking if the new master page should be created from the selected template.

6. Accept the selection by clicking **OK**. The dialog box closes and Flare creates a new master page in the folder **Resources / MasterPages**, which can be accessed from the **Content Explorer**. The new master page is opened in the work space for editing.

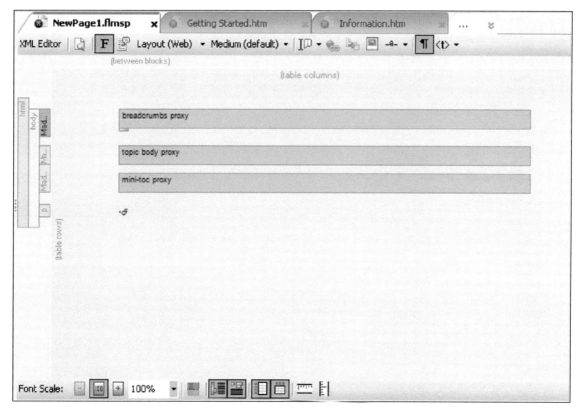

Figure 25: New master page for online help

Editing a Master Page

The master page with predefined content is opened in the editor of Flare after creating a new master page. The master page can be edited like any other topic, for example, the mini-ToC proxy at the bottom of the page can be deleted and replaced by a copyright note. Any changes to the master page take effect only during compilation.

Assigning a Master Page

A master page can be assigned through the target, this applies the master page to all pages, which are connected to this target. See section 5.7.4 "How Everything Comes Together: The Target".

5.7.2   Stylesheets

The stylesheet defines the paragraph and character formatting for the help project. The stylesheet can be used to define the standard font or the color for the various paragraph formats. A stylesheet needs to be assigned to help pages. The effects of the stylesheet are immediately visible while editing the topic files in Flare.

It is possible to use several stylesheets within a project, for example, for different clients, different media (online and print), or for different products that are covered within one project. The format classes are assigned to different categories. The categories allow selecting views for the style classes:

Table 10: Categories for format classes in the stylesheet

Category	Description
Auto-numbered styles	Includes format classes for auto-numbered lists
Topic styles	Includes format classes for the entire topic, e. g. the HTML class
Paragraph styles	Includes format classes for paragraphs, e. g. the standard paragraph p
Footnote styles	Includes format classes for footnotes, e. g. MadCap|footnote
Heading styles	Includes format classes for headings, e. g. the first level heading h1
Character styles	Includes format classes for characters, e. g. bold or monospace
Table styles	Includes format classes for tables
List styles	Includes format classes for lists, e. g. ordered or unordered lists
Link styles	Includes format classes for active and visited links
Dynamic Effects styles	Includes format classes for popups, drop-down text, expanding text
Reusable Content styles	Includes format classes for information blocks, variables, proxies
Generated Content styles	Includes format classes for generated content e. g. glossaries, tables of content, and indices for print output
Controls/Forms styles	Includes format classes for buttons and forms in the help

Any amount of stylesheets can be added and used within a project, but it is also possible to use one stylesheet for different media. By default, the media selection is set to work for both options (**Medium: default**). It is possible to set style properties for the defined media independently (**Medium: non-print** and **Medium: print**).

Importing a Stylesheet

An existing stylesheet, for example, from a different project, can be imported into the current project by following these steps:

1. Select the command **Project > Add Stylesheet**. The dialog box **Add New Stylesheet** opens.

2. Click on the ellipsis (...) button next to the field **Source File**. The dialog box **Open** appears.

3. Select in the dialog box **Open** and then select the path and the stylesheet file.

4. Click on **Open**. The dialog box closes and the new selection shows in the field **Source File**.

5. Enter a new name into **File name** if desired.

6. Click on **Add** to import the stylesheet. A new dialog box opens asking if the stylesheet should be copied into the project.

7. Click **OK** in the confirmation message. The dialog boxes close and Flare copies the stylesheet into the folder **Resources / Stylesheet**, which is accessible through the **Content Explorer**. The stylesheet is then opened in the editor for editing.

Creating a new Stylesheet

Follow these steps for adding a new stylesheet:

1. Select the command **Project > Add Stylesheet**. The dialog box **Add New Stylesheet** opens.

2. If desired, select a template for the stylesheet.

3. Click on **Add** to create the new stylesheet. The dialog box closes and a confirmation message appears asking about copying the new stylesheet to the project using the selected template.

4. Click on **OK**. The dialog box closes and Flare creates the new stylesheet in the folder **Resources / Stylesheets**, which is accessible through the **Content Explorer**.

Figure 26: New stylesheet in advanced view

Display in the Stylesheet Editor

The paragraph and character styles can be edited using a simplified or advanced view. The views can be toggled by clicking on the first button in the local toolbar. Flare saves the current view selection for stylesheets and uses the same view the next time a stylesheet is opened. New stylesheets will also be displayed using the currently selected view.

The advanced view shows the styles and the properties in two lists: on the left are the styles in a hierarchical tree view and on the right are the grouped properties. The selection tools above the lists allow for filtering the styles and properties. The advanced view allows editing of properties of only one style at a time.

The simplified view allows for editing of the most important properties of a style. In the simplified view the properties of several selected styles can be edited at the same time. Select the styles to edit using the mouse while holding down the Shift or Ctrl key. A double-click on the selected styles opens the properties dialog box in which the specific property values can be changed.

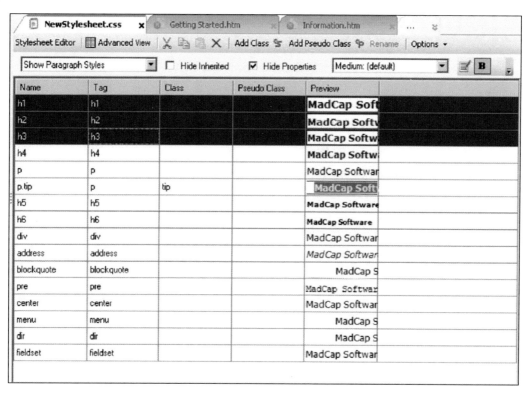

Figure 27: Simplified View of the Stylesheet Editor

Editing a Stylesheet (Advanced View)

1. Select the style category selection to **Show Paragraph Styles**. The list of the style classes now shows only paragraph styles.

2. Select the properties view selection to **Show: Property Groups**.

3. From the list of style classes select style class **H1**. The properties for this style class are shown as groups in the list of properties.

4. Open the property group **Font** by clicking on the plus sign. All properties in a group have a name and a value.

5. Click on the property value **(not set)** of **font-family**. The dialog box **Font Family Picker** opens.

6. Choose **Installed Families** from the list on the left. All fonts that are installed on the system are now shown in the list on the right.

7. Select a font family in the list on the right, for example, Verdana.

8. Accept by clicking **OK**. The dialog box closes and the font family is now used as the value for **font-family**. The file name of the stylesheet displayed in the tab header is now marked with an asterisk indicating that a change took place.

9. Click on the value for the property **font-size**. An arrow appears on the right.

10. Click on the arrow and a dialog box for setting the font size opens.

11. First select the desired unit by clicking on the arrow next to **em**. A list with the available units appears.

12. Select the desired unit, for example, **Point (pt)** for print output or **Pixel (px)** for online output.

13. Next, set the font size for the heading, for example, 14 Point.

14. Accept the change by clicking **OK**. The dialog box closes and the changed value appears for the property **font-size**.

15. Save the stylesheet with the command **File > Save**. The asterisk next to the file name in the tab header disappears.

16. Change any other styles and properties based on the layout requirements.

Assigning a Stylesheet

It is possible to assign a stylesheet to multiple topics, but also multiple stylesheets to one topic. Follow these steps to assign a stylesheet to multiple topics:

1. Select the command **View > File List**. The **File List** opens.

2. Select the topic files which need to have a stylesheet assigned.

3. Click with the right mouse button on this selection and choose the command **Properties**. The dialog box **Properties** opens.

4. Select the tab **Topic Properties**.

5. Select the desired stylesheet from the list **Stylesheet**.

6. Click **OK** to accept the selection.

Follow these steps to assign multiple stylesheets to a topic:

1. Select the **Content Explorer**.

2. Open the topic that needs to have multiple stylesheets assigned.

3. Select the command **Tools > Stylesheet Links**. The dialog box **Stylesheet Links** opens.

4. Select in the list on the right the stylesheets that need to be assigned to the topic.

5. Click on the double arrow button << between the lists to assign the selected stylesheets to the topic.

6. Click **OK** to accept the assignment. The dialog box closes.

Assigning an Individual Style

The different styles from the stylesheet can be assigned either through the format toolbar or through the **Styles** window.

1. Select the **Content Explorer**.

2. Open the topic that needs formatting.

3. Select the command **View > Toolbars > Text Format** or **View > Style Window**. The selected element displays.

4. Select the paragraphs or characters in the topic for formatting. Placing the cursor inside the paragraph is sufficient for marking that paragraph.

5. Select from the tool bar or the **Styles** window the style for the paragraph or character. The format changes based on the selected style.

5.7.3 Skins

A skin defines the appearance and, if applicable, the behavior of the help window. Depending on the help format a skin is more or less configurable and the appearance can differ. The following properties can be set for all three help formats (HTMLHelp, WebHelp, DotNetHelp):

- size and screen position of the help window
- title of the help window
- tools in the toolbar
- elements of navigation (tabs)
- synchronization with the table of contents (the current topic is highlighted in the table of contents in the compiled help)
- commentary feature for Feedback Service

A skin is assigned to the topics through the target, see the section 5.7.4 "How Everything Comes Together: The Target". The effects are visible after compiling the help, see section 3.6.3

"Generating Online Help". A project can make use of several skins, for example, for different clients, different help formats, or different products that are covered in the project.

Creating a Skin

Follow these steps to create a new skin:

1. Select the command **Project > Add Skin**. The dialog box **Add Skin** opens.

2. Select a template for the skin.

3. Enter a name for the skin in **File Name**.

4. Click on **Add** to create the new skin. The dialog box closes and a confirmation dialog box appears asking if the new skin is to be created using the selected template.

5. Accept the selection by clicking **OK**. The dialog box closes and Flare creates the new skin in the folder **Skins**, which is accessible through the **Project Organizer**. The new skin is opened in the editor for editing.

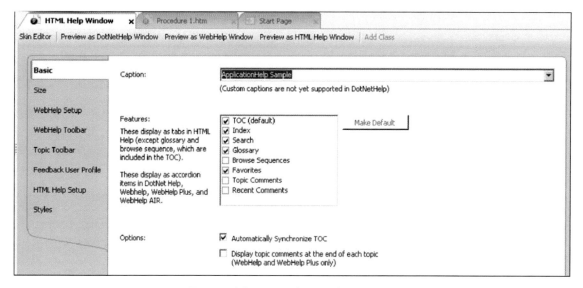

Figure 28: New skin with settings

The MadCap Flare Skin Gallery offers ready-made skins for use with WebHelp, which can be downloaded from here: http://madcapsoftware.com/downloads/flareskingallery.aspx.

Editing a Skin

The local toolbar of the skin editor offers a preview function so that any changes can be reviewed immediately. The settings on the first two tabs **Basic** and **Size** apply to all help formats. The settings on the tab **Styles** only apply to WebHelp and WebHelp Plus.

5.7.4   How Everything Comes Together: The Target

The target is the control file that defines which output format is supposed to get compiled. Targets can be created for the following output formats:

- HTML Help (file extension .chm)
- DotNetHelp
- WebHelp, WebHelp AIR, WebHelp Plus (browser based help)
- Word document
- FrameMaker document or book
- PDF document
- XPS document
- XHTML Book
- DITA

A project can include an unlimited amount of targets for any output format, for example, different targets can be added for help files or books that are geared to different target groups. A target combines layout settings and contents with the output format, for example:

- master page
- page layout
- glossary
- variables

- conditions

This means that anything that influences the compiled output is connected to the target.

Creating a Target

Follow these steps to create a new target:

1. Select the command **Project > Add Target**. The dialog box **Add Target** appears.

2. Select a template for the target from **Templates**.

3. Give the target a name in **File Name**.

4. Click on **Add** to create the new target. The dialog box closes and a confirmation dialog box appears asking if the new target is to be created using the selected template.

5. Accept the selection by clicking **OK**. The dialog box closes and Flare creates the new target in the folder **Targets**, which is accessible through the **Project Organizer**. The new target is opened in the editor for editing.

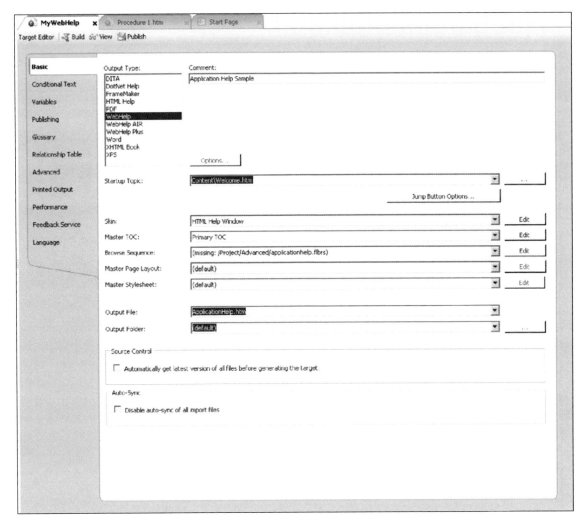

Figure 29: New target for browser based help

The settings in the various tabs determine how the output gets compiled and, if applicable, what will happen to the output after compilation:

Table 11: Tabs in the Target

Tab	Description	Output Format
Basic	General settings for all output formats such as output type and name of the output file or frame set	All

Tab	Description	Output Format
Conditional Text	Defines which topics will be included in the output through conditions, which can be switched on or off	All
Variables	Sets the variable definitions for the output	All
Publishing	Sets the publishing destinations to which the output is to be copied after generation, such as a file server	All
Glossary	Defines which glossaries are to be used for the output	All
Advanced	Controls the layout of the output	All
Printed Output	Defines special options for printed output, for example, that popups are expanded to in-line text	Printed Output
Performance	Defines for WebHelp and DotNetHelp how the table of contents and index are created; these options are especially interesting for complex help systems	WebHelp, DotNetHelp
Feedback Service	Activates the Feedback Service from MadCap	All online help
Language	Sets the language for the output	All

Editing a Target

Follow the steps below for editing a target. As an example the steps cover selection of the skin, setting the media type for output, and the selection of the master page.

1. Change to the **Project Organizer**.

2. Open the folder **Targets**.

3. Double-click on the desired target to open it.

4. Select on the tab **Basic** from the list **Skin** the desired skin.

5. Change to the tab **Advanced**.

6. Select from the list **Master Page** the applicable master page.

7. Select from the list **Stylesheet Medium** the entry **non-print** for online help or **print** for printed output.

8. Save the target with the command **File > Save**.

Setting the Default Target

The compilation of output is controlled and started via the target. Typically, the compilation is initiated from the context menu of the target. It is possible to set one target as a default and then start its compilation by pressing the F6 key.

1. Change to the **Project Organizer**.

2. Open the folder **Targets**.

3. Right-click on the desired target and select from the context menu the command **Make Primary**. The target is now defined as the default and appears in bold font in the folder.

4. Press the F6 key. The default target gets compiled.

5.7.5   Pictures and Video

Flare can import the following picture file formats:

- .bmp
- .gif
- .jpg, .jpeg
- .png
- .tif, .tiff

The supported video file format is .swf.

Inserting a Picture

1. Change to the **Content Explorer**.

2. Open the topic for inserting the picture into by double-clicking.

3. Place the cursor at the location where the picture should be inserted.

4. Select the command **Insert > Picture**. The dialog box **Insert Picture** opens.

5. Select a new picture using **Browse...** or choose one that already exists in the project from the **All images in the project** list.

6. Enter a text for a **Screen Tip** or for **Alternate Text** if desired.

7. Accept the selection by clicking **OK**. The picture is inserted at the cursor position. Flare copies new pictures to the folder **Resources / Images** which is accessible from the **Content Explorer**.

Changing the Picture Dimensions

1. Click on the picture to select it. A symbol appears in the bottom right corner of the picture.

2. Hover the mouse pointer over the symbol and the pointer changes to a cross.

3. Resize the picture by holding the left mouse button down and dragging the corner until the picture has the desired size.

Alternatively, right-click on the picture and select the command **Object...** from the context menu. The dimensions can then be specified on the **Size** and **Print Size** tabs in the **Media Properties** dialog box.

Movies and Sounds

Movies and sounds can be added to topics through the use of these additional products from MadCap:

- Mimic for movies
- Echo for sounds

6 Navigation

Traditional texts are organized linearly. They are supposed to be read in a specific sequence by stringing paragraphs together, this means reading from the first to the last page. Readers always have various reading alternatives in non-linear hypertexts: the reader can choose which topic to read next. This means that hypertexts have no defined reading sequence. Regular texts have a sequential array of paragraphs, but this physical structure does not follow the logical structure, which is typically hierarchical and uses cross-references.

The main problem with hypertexts or hypermedia applications is the orientation in complex and manifold networked information systems and thus the navigation. Often enough the user can no longer recall how he or she got to the current page or how to get back to a previously viewed page because the user traversed many levels of the system by clicking on many links and then looses the orientation more and more.

In this case it is no longer a targeted search, but the user meanders around in the system and tries to regain the overview (lost in hyperspace). An aberration in the system can also lead to useful information and surprising cross-connections by accident, which fits the current learning process (serendipity).

6.1 Problems with Orientation

The orientation problem and the closely related problem of cognitive overload are even today considered unsolved problems of hypertext technology. A large amount of research is dedicated to these two problems. The orientation problem can be split into several sub-problems:

The users do not know,

- where they are in relation to the other information in the hypertext;

- how they can get to a specific piece of information, which they assume is in the hypertext;

- how to find the best entrance point to the hypertext, where the best start point is;

- how to return to a specific location which was visited previously,

- what the best path through the hypertext is in regards to the question a user has;

- if they really saw all relevant information;

- how complex the hypertext is and which information it contains;

- what they can do at their current location and where they can go from there.

Some of these problems are also observed during reading of traditional linear books, especially when the books are not structured well or have an insufficient table of contents or index. Also, readers of books can have problems with finding a spot again or trying to gauge if a specific piece of information is included in the text.

Other problems are more specific to hypertext. For example, readers of linear texts will not have the problem of knowing what they can do at any given point because the only options are forwards or backwards. When users read an entire book they know that they are supposed to read all pages. Furthermore, it is unproblematic for readers to determine the amount of text of traditional books as opposed to determining the amount of hypertexts.

Books have more orientation guides than hypertexts. Book orientation guides became intuitive because of their frequent use. For example, page numbers as well as the thickness of the left and right portion of the book give a clue about one's relative position within a book. The cover of an already read book (new, worn, color, etc) allows for fast location of the book among others, and the page layout (footnotes, pictures, headings, etc) makes finding specific information within the book easier by using visual cues.

Additional confusion in hypertexts can be caused by multiple links, for example, when the same page can be reached through various paths within the system, but the content of the page does not accommodate for that. The individual pages have to be within a meaningful context. Remarks such as "see above" or "compare to the previous page" relate only to a specific preceding page. This confuses the reader and the reader may get the impression he or she has missed something.

6.2 Finding Information

Browsing and navigating are the most important activities within hypertexts. Browsing turns into navigating the more the readers know about the set of information, which means they developed a good idea about the relationship of the individual topics to each other. The navigation in hypertexts is often compared to navigation in a natural environment.

Readers can access information in hypertexts in three ways:

- through links
- through full text search
- through navigational tools in the browser (table of contents and index)

Links are an additional option to find information besides using the traditional search mechanisms (entry of search term and their logical connection). Readers often do not know exactly what they are searching for and thus cannot craft that into a suitable query. Links offer, in this case, a more flexible opportunity for searching information; users do not have to plan the search beforehand, but they can browse freely through the set of information. This suits people with hovering attention better.

The full text search is one of the most important access strategies besides the hypertext-specific access mechanism of links. Searching is a time saver, when the user can clearly formulate the search term and the connection of the desired information with its context is not necessary.

The third way of accessing information in hypertexts is through the navigational tools in the help window (browser). A topic is clicked on directly in the browser (for example in the table of contents or index) and then immediately displayed on screen. The access of information contained in online help is further differentiated between context sensitive and context free.

Context Sensitive

Context sensitive help shows the user the information that applies to the current situation within the product. The user does not have to search for the information. The context can refer to three different levels:

- dialog box level: information for the current dialog box, window, or tab. Help is called through a help button, a help link, or a press on the F1 key.

- element level: information at the field or element level. Help is called, for example, through the movable question mark symbol.

- embedded help: short texts and instructions that are integrated into the user interface.

Context Free

This access method opens an independent online help without any relation to the current state of the product. The context free help is typically accessed through the help menu. The user can access the context free help indirectly as well as after a context sensitive help call, for example, a dialog box description, or through a help agent. Then the user needs the tools mentioned before to find the information.

6.3   Navigational Tools

The orientation problem has different causes and as a result different navigational tools were developed, which can remedy one or more of the problem causes. This is why hypertexts often have a combination of navigational assistants.

6.3.1 Traditional Orientation Guides

Traditional orientation guides are meta-information that are also used in books and transferred to the hypertext concept. Traditional orientation guides show the text structure and help with finding information quickly.

6.3.1.1 *Table of Contents*

Tables of contents in books are intended to give the reader a high level overview of the contents and the hierarchical structure of the text. Additionally, by using page numbers, a table of contents allows for targeted access to specific text passages.

A table of contents allows for directly accessing topics in a hypertext by clicking on the specific entry. The table of contents provides for a logical and often hierarchical overview of the hypertext. The display of this hierarchy is, in the current state-of-the-art technology, an expandable and collapsible tree view. The logical structure is based on the viewpoint of the author and does not necessarily have to be the same logical viewpoint of the user.

Not every topic has to be listed in the table of contents, but every topic has to be accessible through a topic listed in the table of contents. Whether all or only the most important topics are listed in the table of contents depends on several criteria:

- extent of the online help
- distribution of information across the topics
- alternative means of access for the topics not listed in the table of contents

Whether all-inclusive or not, the main goal of a table of contents is to have clarity and manageability. Only then the table of contents will provide the users with orientation. This is achieved through:

- outline of the table of contents
- limited outline depth

- clarity of entries

- alerts

Alerts can be linguistic or graphical. The reader should be able to gain knowledge about which topic classes can be expected based on the entries in the table of contents. For example, topics with instructions can always start or end with a verb to indicate the task: "Saving of files" or "File saving". The list of instructions (1., 2., 3., etc.) can also be illustrated by using a symbol that is used to prefix the topic entries in the table of contents.

A special table of contents type is the so called **breadcrumbs** inside of a topic. For example, breadcrumbs that are shown as a path. They are intended to reduce complex hypertext structures to a minimum of text. The breadcrumbs are a metaphor of the fairy tale of Hansel and Gretel, who left breadcrumbs behind to find their way home.

A synchronization of the currently displayed topic with the entry in the table of contents is also very helpful. Topics that were accessed through links are highlighted in the table of contents to indicate the context in which the topic is placed.

6.3.1.2 Index

The reader can use the index in a book to systematically search for content. The reader can find specific text passages through the page numbers of the entries in the index. The index in a hypertext allows direct access of a topic by clicking on the entry. The index provides a guided search in contrast to a full text search. The guided search is defined by the author. This means that the reader cannot find terms that the author did not add to the index. The viewpoint of the author may not be the same viewpoint of the reader.

The index does not need to include every topic, but it should contain:

- terms used in the user interface

- terms used in the help system, including those from the introduction, the safety advisories, and notes and tips

- permuted entries, such as "save file" as well as "file, save"

- terms for beginners as well as experts

- common terms that are typically used by the users

- synonyms that are likely to be used by the users (such as "save file" and "store file")

6.3.1.3 *Glossary*

Every well-written reference book contains a glossary. It provides short explanations and definitions of the technical terms used in the text as well as references to the locations where the terms are used.

Hypertexts may contain various types of dynamic glossaries. For example, when clicking on a term a window (popup) with a definition opens. Besides that, the popup may include references to other sections that are relevant for the term. The applicable topic is shown in the help window when such a reference is clicked in the glossary.

The glossary can also be an alphabetical list of all terms in the glossary. A click on an entry directly shows the explanation or opens a special glossary window.

6.3.2 Orientation through Limitation

Orientation problems can be reduced by lowering the complexity of the hypertext structure. The users then work within partial structures. Various options are available for this approach.

Browse Sequences

Browse sequences are paths through the hypertext network that the author selects. Browse sequences reduce extensive and complex hypertext structures to interesting or central contents in order to provide the reader with better navigation. Browse sequences are a type of superlink that not only connect two topics, but an entire topic sequence. Browse sequences have very simple link patterns and are usually linear.

Readers can access browse sequences through special buttons or commands. The reader can navigate with forward and back buttons within a browse-sequence. A browse-sequence should further allow readers to access topics outside of the browse sequence through links.

Browse sequences are not navigational tools in the traditional sense because they make navigation unnecessary. Similar to traditional texts browse sequences only have a forward and backward direction. Browse sequences are a linear path through a non-linear hypertext. Although browse sequences eliminate the orientation problem and make navigation unnecessary, they go directly back to linear texts. The question is what is left from the non-linear hypertext concept when the solution to the orientation problem is the creation of linearity.

Individual and Dynamically Generated Paths

Besides browse sequences that are defined by the author, are paths that are created during navigation. The information of interest can be collected, filtered, associatively linked, and permanently stored in a collection of data. The paths can also be generated by the system based on a search query of the user. This mechanism is a compromise between the traditional methods of full text search (listing of search results) and free navigation in hypertexts.

Hypertrails

Hypertrails are more complex restrictions to the hypertext structure in contrast to browse sequences, which use very simple link structures. Hypertrails create a substructure out of all topic links, which is structured exclusively for one aspect of a subject. Hypertrails provide various, but still structured views for different contents, target groups, and tasks. Hypertrails allow for creating multi-dimensional hypertexts, in which information can be structured differently based on various requirements.

Filter

Filters can reduce a very complex topic link structure to a substructure that is of current interest in a hypertext session. These filters can act as a search query, such as "show all topics, that have ...". The user then sees only the filtered topics and links and can navigate only within this selection. Filters can also be implemented in such a way that only specific links are shown when the hypertext contains typified links.

6.3.3 Reverse Orientation Assistance

Reverse orientation assistance is intended to prevent those orientation problems that are described by the questions: "How did I get here? How do I get back to a location visited previously?". These types of navigational tools are realized by capturing a history in the computer system.

Backtracking

Backtracking is an important navigational tool and is supported by most hypertext systems. Users can click on the back button of the browser and through this backtracking retrace their path through the hypertext network step by step. The topics are accessed one after another in the reverse sequence. Readers can retrace the path until they find a familiar topic or reach the beginning if they encounter orientation problems. Backtracking should always be available and always be initiated the same way. The recording of the path should always reach back to the beginning.

Backtracking can be a problem for inexperienced hypertext users because there is no such counterpart in linear texts. When a hypertext offers the option to browse back and forth within a browse sequence as well as backtracking, users can get confused because they do not understand the difference between backtracking and browsing back in a browse-sequence.

The browse back button for a browse-sequence returns the user to the topic that is placed in the browse sequence before the current topic, while clicking the button for backtracking displays the topic viewed previously. When the difference between these two functions is not implemented in an obvious way it may send readers to a topic that they may have never seen before. This shows that the book metaphor insufficiently represents hypertext-specific concepts.

History List

A history list is a special function that automatically lists all previously visited topics in sequence. The difference between a history list and backtracking is that a history list allows one to access already visited topics directly by clicking on the name or applicable row in the history list.

History lists can be saved temporarily, this means for the duration of the session, or permanently. It is recommended to store date, time, and list name when saving a history list permanently. Some browsers offer, besides the backwards / forwards function, history list management. This allows one to influence the display of the previously visited topics, for example, based on date or site.

Favorites

Saving favorites (setting bookmarks) is an active navigational tool. The reader can mark interesting topics and view or print them easily at a later point in time.

Home

The home button sends the reader back to the topic that the technical writer defined as the start topic, or it returns the reader to a starting point.

6.4 Links

Links create a relationship between topics. Users can navigate the information network only through links. Links and topics together create the typical, non-linear hypertext structure. All links have a start and end point, also called source and destination anchor. In literature the source anchors are also called references, link points, link indicators, link icons, hot words, hotspots, or buttons. Destination anchors are also known as link regions, destination points, or reference points.

6.4.1 Types of Links

Links can be unidirectional or bidirectional. Most hypertext systems support links only in one direction, from the source anchor to the destination anchor. Bidirectional links are supported typically only through the browse back function. This means that the opposite way is only available when a link was accessed going forward. Links can also be **intra-, inter-,** and **extra-hypertextual**. Intra-hypertextual links connect two sections within a topic. This type of link is used when the topic content is very complex and cannot be shown entirely in the help window.

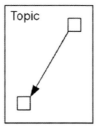

Figure 30: Intra-hypertextual link

A special form of intra-hypertextual links in online help are information blocks that can be shown and hidden. These blocks are hidden when accessing the topic and require a click on a sensitive element to be shown. Information blocks that can be shown and hidden can be displayed in various ways:

- popup: the information, typically an image or an explanation of a term, is shown in a small window. The popup opens in proximity to the sensitive element.

- expandable text: the information is shown on the right side of the sensitive element.

- drop-down text: the information is shown below the sensitive element.

Inter-hypertextual links connect two topics of the same hypertext document. Inter-hypertextual links are the most common links in online help. Usually, the current topic content of the help window is replaced with the new topic content. The new content can also be displayed in another window, called secondary window.

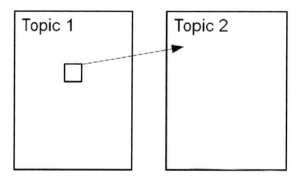

Figure 31: Inter-hypertextual link

A special form of the inter-hypertextual links in online help are image maps. An image map consist of an image where sections are turned into sensitive areas, which then link to the applicable content. Image maps are well suited as navigational tool in a context-free help system for a complex software product. Links to movies or audio files are also considered inter-hypertextual links.

Extra-hypertextual links connect two topics from different hypertexts. For example, the following items can be accessed through extra-hypertextual links:

- a topic in a different online help system

- a web site

- a file (for example a PDF document)

When using these links the content of the help window can either be replaced by the new content or the new content can be shown in a secondary window.

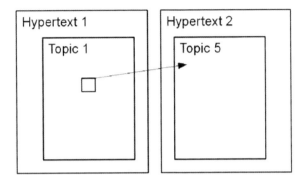

Figure 32: Extra-hypertextual link

Secondary windows have the advantage that the user can view all information on screen; the context of the source anchor is not lost. The disadvantage of secondary windows, as well as for popups, is that they can overlay relevant information in the primary window, negating the advantage. Usability tests have shown that users get confused when too many windows are open and that the users are not always aware of how to close the popups or secondary windows.

Links can also be differentiated based on the globality or locality of their source and destination anchors. A global anchor is an entire topic, a local anchor is a specific region within a topic (bookmark). This results in four possible combinations of the global and local source and destination anchors, shown in figure 33.

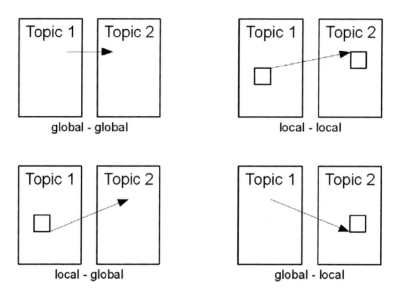

Figure 33: Global and local anchors

Local destination anchors can be realized in a topic through bookmarks. Links have in most cases a local source anchor and a global destination anchor. This type of reference is common in books, for example, references to previous or upcoming articles in foot notes. The most important differentiation, which can be further differentiated as needed, is the differentiation between referential and typified links.

6.4.1.1 Referential Links

Referential links or associative references are the most common and typical links in hypertexts. They create a relationship between topics without explicitly specifying the type of relationship although the topics are related contextually. However, referential links are not created arbitrarily.

Referential links are often links for which a term is used as a source anchor. Such a link most often references a topic that contains more information about the term. A special form of associative references are annotations, which are not considered as self-contained and independent units. They only make sense in combination with the referencing unit. Annotations are not stored in separate hypertext topics, but are displayed temporarily in a separate window next to or above the current text.

6.4.1.2 Typified Links

Typified links are references that specify the relationship between two topics. They are used for structuring hypertexts and are also called structural, organized, or organizational links. Jeff Conklin defines "organizational links" as links that create a hierarchical structure in the sense of "is-a"-relationships.

Hypertexts are not entirely without structure. They also often have, besides associative references, typified links, which provide for a structure based on the text content. Depending on the scope, special link types are provided in order to clarify the structure for the users.

6.4.1.3 Interactive Elements

Interactive elements (shortcuts) are a direct link with the graphical user interface being described. They are typically displayed with a special button or symbol. For example, a click on an interactive element can open the described dialog box in the application in one step. This saves users complicated navigation inside an application, and it saves the technical writer from having to provide information that is directly available from the dialog box.

Interactive elements are not intended to replace a step in the description or the entire procedure. Users need the information about how to reach that dialog box in the application. Interactive elements are only available in HTMLHelp.

6.4.2 Display and Placement of Link Anchors

Hypertexts provide for many different methods of placing and displaying link anchors. Links can be integrated in text or separated from it. Links are called embedded links when they are integrated into the text. One technique for displaying these embedded links is marking a word, the so called hotspot. This marking is usually displayed by using a specific font color and underlining of the word. The link anchor is in this case the word itself. In order to reach the topic that is referenced by the anchor the user has to click on the marked word. An embedded link can also be displayed by a symbol prefix or suffix that indicates the link anchor. Sensitive and interactive elements make use of this technique.

Hotspots are not marked in some hypertexts, but the shape of the cursor is changed when hovering over the hotspot. The advantage of the invisible link anchor is that the flow of reading is not disturbed by the emphasis of the word. The permanent marking of embedded links can be very disturbing for the reading process when a topic contains many links of various types. A strong disadvantage of invisible links is that many readers do not notice these links and thus cannot make use of them.

A link gets the highest attention when it is placed inside of the text, assuming that the font color is chosen appropriately and that there are not too many links. A smart placement of links takes the reader by the hand and guides him through the hypertext. Nevertheless, the reader is still free to decide not to follow the link, but it is well possible that browse-happy readers will navigate away from the desired content due to the heightened attention.

Some hypertexts have a strict separation between the text and the links. The links can either be displayed at all times or need to be explicitly enabled by the user, for example, by clicking on a button. This is called a link bundle or "See also"-links.

An advantage of such link bundling is that many users know this way of interaction from other applications. The disadvantage of such separation is that readers are less inclined to follow these links. This lack of willingness can also seen as advantage because it saves the readers partially or entirely from chaotically navigating through the hypertext.

6.5 *Conclusion for Online Help*

Online help displayed in a help window comes with a built-in navigation that is already configured. The quasi-standard help window determines important sections of online help that the technical writer does not have to worry about: the navigation on the left side of the help window and the tool bar at the top. The content displayed here is determined by the properties of the help window. Reverse orientation assistance is also implemented in large part as a property of help windows.

The partitioning of the help window of HTMLHelp, and thus the position of the navigation, cannot be changed. In a browser based help system almost everything can be changed because the components are HTML frames. The type of navigation is defined by the technical writer through compilation, for example, a two-tiered index through the compilation of index entries.

Full text search is also a property of the help window that can be enabled. Words can be excluded from the search database because some words do not make much sense on their own, such as "the", "a", or "and". These words are collected in a list, the so called stop word list.

Flare can exclude individual topics from search through a setting in the topic properties, for example, those topics that are supposed to be displayed only as popups.

6.5.1 Traditional Orientation Assistance

Traditional orientation assistance, such as table of contents or index, is the backbone of navigation of online help. Besides full-text search, traditional orientation assistance offers the most entry points into context-free help..

6.5.1.1 *Table of Contents*

A table of contents should be available in any online help with two or more topics. It defines a logical, hierarchical structure of the networked topics and offers direct access to the individual pieces of information. The task of the technical writer is to craft a table of contents that is not too detailed, but also not too broad. A structure of not more than four levels deep with about seven topics each is recommended. This, for sure, is a challenge for online help for more complex products and shows why not all topics have to be in the table of contents, but can be made accessible through links.

There are various options of structuring a table of contents. One can follow the topic classification and separate those based on a target group or process:

- concept topics (information geared towards learning)

- procedure topics (information geared towards tasks)

- reference topics (information geared towards functions)

One variation is to structure topics based on target groups at the top level and then assign those the applicable topic classes.

The structural levels of a tree structure in a table of contents (books) can also be associated with a topic. This topic is displayed when the user clicks on the book in the table of contents. There are pros and cons to this approach. One general recommendation for this method is consistency. Otherwise, the user has to try out each book to see if a topic is linked to it to find out if there is relevant information or not.

In this context Flare has one peculiarity: when the books are linked to topics the elements of breadcrumbs become sensitive and the reader can use them for navigation. Ideally, the table of contents is synchronized with the displayed topic and the topics contain breadcrumbs so that the user can always determine the current position within the online help.

6.5.1.2 *Index*

An index is necessary when the online help is larger than ten topics. In each topic that is accessible from the index two to five index entries should exist. A two-tiered index is proven to work well.

An index entry should consist of as few as possible, meaningful words. Entries that are not meaningful on their own or are ambiguous should have several sub-entries. When an entry generates more than ten hits it should be split into several entries. The following table gives an overview of possible index entries and their typical use:

Table 12: Types of index entries

Index Entry	Format	Example

Noun	<ul><li>without article and singular</li><li>use plural form only when there is no singular or if an amount is meant</li></ul>	File
		File name extensions
		    .flrpj
		    .htm
		    .mpj

Adjective	base form	external
		    link
		    variable
		...
		link
		    external
		    internal

Verb	infinitive	file save ... save file
Abbreviation Unabridged version	commonly used form, all other forms are listed as "see also" reference	

Style guides and formatting rules for index entries are especially important when multiple writers work on a help project. These should include, for example:

- capitalization of verbs and adjectives, for example always capitalize, capitalize only for the first tier, or based on the word form

- use of singular and plural

- handling of a term in different contexts

- minimum amount of sub-entries per index entry

- maximum amount of sub-entries per index entry

An index entry can produce hits for one or more topics. These topics will be shown in the online help system as a menu from which the user can selected the desired topic. The entries in this menu are based on the topic titles, see section "4.5.3 Topic Properties".

6.5.1.3 Glossary

Starting with three or four technical terms in an online help, a glossary should be present. A glossary is a collection of all special terms and their definitions. It contains all words that require explanation, such as:

- technical terms

- foreign words

- acronyms and abbreviations

An online help can have a central glossary or contain explanations for special terms directly inside of the topic. Possible approaches for this are:

- popups

- expanding text

6.5.2 Restrictions

Browse sequences have gone a bit out of style. They are useful for special target groups such as novices, or for important processes. Browse sequences are recommended when the users have to read or work off of information (for example about sub-tasks) in a specific order. Browse sequences have to

- be clearly identifiable,

- have an obvious start and end.

The first version of HTMLHelp allowed technical writers to assign topics in the online help via information types, for example, to special target groups or product variants. An information type acted like a filter that the writer put on top of the hypertext network. The user could then select from a dialog box in which portions of the online help get displayed. This type of filter is no longer supported in the current version of HTMLHelp so that a technical writer has to define filters, for example, through the table of contents or by target group oriented help. Other restrictions, such as hypertrails, cannot be implemented in online help without great difficulty.

6.5.3 Backward Facing Orientation Assistance

Most of backward facing orientation assistance is provided through the help window, for example, the use of favorites or the home button.

6.5.4 Links

Hyperlinks in help text provide the user with fast access to further information. They provide technical writers the opportunity to keep a topic short, to focus on core information, and provide alternative access to additional information. Sensitive elements, such as drop-down text information, can be arranged in levels. Users do not have to leave the context and can access additional information at the click of a button.

Online help can have the following types of links:

Table 13: Types of links

Link Type	Explanation
Jump	Within the primary help window: content is moved or replaced; to secondary window: the context remains in place, e. g. for examples or procedures; possible are internal jumps (within the online help) or external jumps (to a target outside of the online help)
Topic popup	Normal topic that is displayed in a secondary window, e. g. for additional explanations or examples

Link Type	Explanation
Text popup	Text that is displayed in a special text window, similar to tool tips, e. g. for technical terms or abbreviations
Link bundles	Meaningful links to related topics, e. g. "see also" links
Relationship tables	Tables that contain links between different topic classes
Expanding text	Text is shown after the sensitive area (hotspot), e. g. for short explanations or abbreviations
Drop-down text	Text is shown below the sensitive area, e. g. for additional information
Image map	A graphic with sensitive elements, e. g. for orientation in complex systems
Interactive element	(only HTMLHelp) direct connection to the described application

Since there are that many types of links it is recommended one chooses a few selected types. Furthermore, user interfaces and online helps are subject to trends and new findings of usability tests. When graphical user interfaces were first used it was especially modern and considered user friendly to have multiple windows and popups. Today, expanding and drop-down texts are more commonly used. Usability tests showed that users are easily confused by too many open windows and also have problems closing the opened windows.

Although links generate a lot of attention within the text they also have disadvantages: the extra attention leads the users to follow the links without reading the surrounding text. The users navigate away from the information they found without even noticing. Other users are afraid of loosing the information they found and decide not to follow any links. Both approaches sometimes cause a dilemma for the reader.

The solution is a transparent link concept that the users can learn quickly and that they can use as guidance. The requirement is that the link concept is consistently used across the entire online help.

The basis for such a link concept can be the following rules:

- allowed types of links within a topic

- position of links within a topic

- maximum and minimum amount of links per topic

- allowed link types between topic classes

- allowed topic classes for links

For example, links can be bundled in one place within a topic (see section 6.6.6 "See also" Links), and within the text only expanding or drop-down text is used. Other online helps use links and popups sparingly, but notify the user via tool tips or symbols of what will happen when they click on a link.

The following means of displaying a link are confusing to users:

- graphic link that cannot be identified as such

- pseudo-links, underlined text which is not a hyperlink

- image maps when there are alternatives

- clickable bullet points or marks in front of the text

- too many links in the text

- no links within a topic (unintentional dead end)

- repeating the same links within a topic

The source anchors of links should be meaningful so that the user can get an impression of what information to expect. The phrasing can indicate to the reader if a description or task instructions can be expected. The source anchors should consist of more than one word because it improves accessibility. Users often scan topics only for source anchors. If the source anchor consists only of one word the context has to be read and that hinders quick scanning. Additionally, users who are limited in motor function may have difficulty with clicking on an anchor that consists of only one word.

Jumps and popups should be marked differently so that the reader knows what will happen after clicking. This reduces the user's worry of getting lost in the hypertext and being unable to find the information again.

The de-facto standard of the Web defines that hyperlinks are blue and visited links are purple. When the layout of the online help diverges from this standard the visited links should be displayed noticeable different than unvisited links, otherwise readers are loosing an important orientation tool.

6.6   Implementation with Flare

Flare supports all described orientation assistance and link types.

6.6.1   Table of Contents

The table of contents places a hierarchical structure over the topics of an online help. All topics of a Flare project are built into an online help. Topics that are not supposed to be included in the build have to be excluded using conditions. When building a print version only those topics are included in the build that are listed in the table of contents.

Flare allows for creating as many tables of contents as desired, which then can be used to control several output variations. Which table of contents Flare uses for the build is configured in the target, see "Editing a Target" in section 5.7.4 "How Everything Comes Together: The Target".

Creating a new Table of Contents

1. Select from the **Project** menu the command **Add Table of Content...** .The dialog box **Add TOC** appears.

2. Select a different template for the table of contents if desired.

3. Enter a name for the new file into **File Name**.

4. Click on **Add**. A confirmation message appears asking if the new table of contents should be created from the selected template.

5. Click **OK** in the confirmation message. The confirmation message and the dialog box close. Flare creates a new table of contents in the folder **TOCs** in the **Project Organizer** and opens it for editing. The file has an extension of .fltoc.

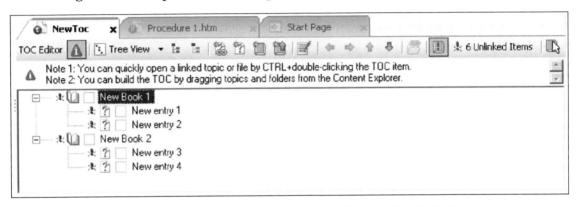

Figure 34: A new table of contents in hierarchical display

Editing a Table of Contents

Flare creates a new table of contents with two books and two topics under each to illustrate a possible structure. Exclamation marks in front of the entries in the table of contents indicate missing links for the specific entries.

Flare offers two different forms of display for editing a table of contents: a hierarchical and a tabular view. Toggling between both views is possible by clicking on the second button in the local tool bar.

The hierarchical view is better suited for creating a table of contents whereas the tabular view is better for editing individual settings, for example, for conditions.

Follow these steps to edit a table of contents:

1. Double-click on the table of contents to edit.

2. Turn the tree view on using the option in the local tool bar.

3. Create new books if needed using the local tool bar.

4. Drag the books to a new position if needed using the mouse.

5. If needed change to the **Content Explorer**.

6. With the mouse, drag topics from the **Content Explorer** to the desired place in the table of contents.

7. Save the table of contents with the command **Save** from the **File** menu.

6.6.1.1 Breadcrumbs

The breadcrumbs are generated by the breadcrumbs proxy, which is configured on the master page, see "Editing a Master Page" in section 5.7.1 "Master Pages". The breadcrumbs proxy works off the topic titles, which are set in the topic properties, see section 4.5.3 "Topic Properties". When no topic title is set, the sections of the breadcrumbs are generated from the first headings of the topics.

This means that one has to enter a topic title for every topic or leave all topic titles blank so that the breadcrumbs are cleanly generated. When creating a help project through import from Word or FrameMaker files, the topic titles are based on the headings for each topic. Creating new topics in Flare does not automatically fill in a topic title. When no title is entered it will default to the text of the first heading in the topic.

Synchronization with the Table of Contents

The automatic synchronization between currently viewed topic and its entry in the table of contents is configured in the skin, see "Editing a Skin" in section 5.7.3 "Skins".

6.6.2 Index

Flare manages index entries at the topic level. This means that there is no single file within the project that contains the index entries, but it exists only after the online help is built. Flare displays index entries as tags. The position of an index entry within the topic is of importance because when clicking on the keyword in the index, the beginning of the paragraph is shown in which the index entry was placed.

Since the index entries are managed within the topics one does not have to connect the target with an index. The content of the index is controlled through the topics in the online help.

Adding an individual Index Entry

1. Change to the **Content Explorer**.

2. Open the topic in which the index entry is to be placed via double-click.

3. Highlight the word in the topic.

4. Press the **F10** key. Flare inserts the highlighted word as index marker in front of the word.

Adding multiple Index Entries

1. Change to the **Content Explorer**.

2. Open the topic in which the index entry is to be placed via double-click.

3. Select from the menus **Tools** > **Index** the command **Index Entry Window**. The **Index Entry** dialog box appears and opens on the right side of the Flare main window.

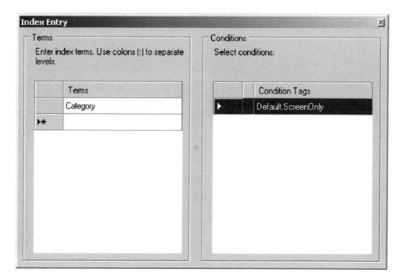

Figure 35: Index Entry editor

4. Place the cursor at the position where the new index entries are to be entered.

5. Type an index key word into the list **Terms** in the **Index Entry** dialog box. The first hierarchical level is separated from the second by using a colon without spaces, for example, File:save.

6. Finalize the key word entry with the Enter key. Flare inserts the index key word as an index marker. The cursor is placed automatically into the second row of the **Terms** list in the **Index Entry** dialog box.

7. Apply condition tags in **Conditions** as desired.

Editing an Index Entry

1. Change to the **Content Explorer**.

2. Open the topic in which the index entry is to be placed via double-click.

3. Click on an index marker and select from the context menu the command **Select**. The marker is now selected and the content is shown in the **Index Entry** dialog box if the dialog box is open. The marker can now be deleted or edited.

Editing an Index

Flare provides the **Index Explorer,** which displays all index key words of the project. Select from the menu **View** the command **Index Explorer** to view it.

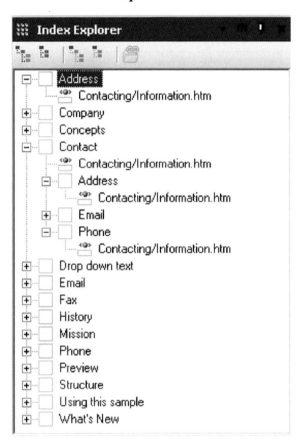

Figure 36: Index Explorer

The Index Explorer shows all levels and entries of the future index. Under each entry are the topics in which the entry is located. The specific topic is opened via double-click. The index markers are edited as usual, see "Editing an Index Entry" in this section.

6.6.3   Glossary

The display of the glossary in the compiled online help is dependent on the help format:

- HTMLHelp: Entry in the table of contents. When done this way, no additional library is needed when employing the online help.

- WebHelp: Tab in the navigation pane of the online help.

- DotNetHelp: Tab in the navigation pane of the online help.

A Flare project can contain as many glossaries as desired so that they can be used for different outputs. Which glossary Flare uses for an output is defined in the target, see "Assigning a Glossary" later on in this section.

Creating a new Glossary

1. Select from the **Project** menu the command **Add Glossary**. The dialog box **Add Glossary** opens.

2. Select a different template for the glossary if desired.

3. Enter a new name for the glossary file into **File Name**.

4. Click **Add**. A confirmation message appears asking if the selected template is to be used for the new glossary.

5. Accept the selection with **OK**. The dialog boxes close, Flare places the new glossary file in the folder **Glossaries** in the **Project Organizer**, and opens it for editing. The file has a name extension of .flglo.

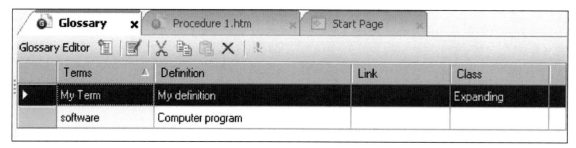

Figure 37: New Glossary

Editing a Glossary

The glossary entries are listed in alphabetical order in the glossary. The properties of a glossary entry are shown in the columns **Definition**, **Link**, and **Class**. New glossary entries are created by clicking on the first icon in the local tool bar.

1. Click on in the local tool bar or double-click on an entry in the glossary table. The **Properties** dialog box opens for the glossary entry.

2. Enter or edit the entry on the tab **Glossary Term**.

3. Enter the applicable explanation into the section **Definition** or select a topic that contains the definition.

4. Specify on the tab **Style** how the term is to be presented within a topic.

5. Click **OK** to accept the entries and settings. The glossary term and its properties are added to the table.

6. Save the glossary file by opening the **File** menu and selecting **Save**.

Activating a Glossary for Online Help

A glossary is not a basic component of a help window. The glossary has to be activated for display in the skin.

1. Change to the **Project Organizer**.

2. Select the folder **Skins** and open the applicable skin via double-click.

3. Chose the **Basic** tab and select from the **Features** list the **Glossary** entry.

4. Save the skin by opening the **File** menu and selecting **Save**.

Assigning a Glossary

In order to have glossaries be part of an output they have to be assigned in the target. This also allows one to select how the glossary terms are to be treated within a topic.

1. Change to the **Project Organizer**.

2. Open the folder **Targets** and open the applicable target via double-click. The target opens for editing.

3. Select on the **Glossary** tab in the section **Glossary Term Conversion** the desired option for treating glossary terms that Flare finds in topics when building the output:

Do not convert terms	The terms are not converted. This option is especially suitable for print output.
Convert only marked terms	Only those terms that were marked and entered as glossary terms are converted based on the style class assigned in the properties for the term.
Convert first occurrence of term	Every first occurrence of a glossary term in a topic is converted based on the style class assigned in the properties for the term.
Convert all occurrences of term	Every occurrence of a glossary term in a topic is converted based on the style class assigned in the properties for the term.

4. Choose in **Select Glossaries To Use When Generating Output** the glossaries that are to be included in the output.

5. Select a **Master Page** for the glossary if desired.

6. Save the target by opening the **File** menu and choosing the command **Save**.

6.6.4 Browse Sequences

The way browse sequences are displayed in the compiled online help depends on the help format:

HTMLHelp   Last entry in the table of contents. This way no additional library is needed when deploying the online help.

WebHelp   Tab in the navigation pane of the online help.

DotNetHelp Tab in the navigation pane of the online help.

Creating a Browse Sequence

1. Change to the **Project Organizer**.

2. Select from the **Project** menu the entry **Advanced** and from there the command **Add Browse Sequence**. The dialog box **Add Browse Sequence** opens.

3. Select a different template for the browse sequence if desired.

4. Enter a name for the browse sequence file in **File Name**.

5. Click on **Add**. A confirmation message appears asking if the selected template is to be used for the new browse sequence.

6. Accept the selection with **OK**. The dialog boxes close, Flare places the new browse sequence file into the folder **Advanced** in the **Project Organizer** (node icon "B"). The browse sequence file name has the extension .flbrs.

A browse sequence can be edited in the same way as a table of contents, see "Editing a Table of Contents" in section 6.6.1 "Table of Contents".

Activating a Browse Sequence for Online Help

A browse sequence is not a basic component of a help window. The browse sequence has to be activated for display in the skin.

1. Change to the **Project Organizer**.

2. Select the folder **Skins** and open the applicable skin via double-click.

3. Chose the **Basic** tab and select from the **Features** list the **Browse Sequences** entry.

4. Save the skin by opening the **File** menu and selecting **Save**.

6.6.5 Links

Most of the links can be used for topics and files (global) as well as for bookmarks within topics (local). This is why the first description is about creating a bookmark.

6.6.5.1 *Creating Bookmarks*

1. Switch to the **Content Explorer**.

2. Double-click on the topic in which the bookmark needs to be placed.

3. Set the cursor at the position where the bookmark needs to be placed.

4. Select from the **Insert** menu the command **Bookmark**. The dialog box **Manage Bookmarks** opens.

5. Enter a name into the field **New bookmark**.

6. Click on **Add** to accept the settings. The dialog box closes and the bookmark is added at the current cursor position. The bookmark is shown with a flag symbol when the markers are set to be displayed (select from the **View** menu the entry **Show** and in there the command **Show Markers**).

7. Save the topic by opening the **File** menu and selecting the **Save** command.

6.6.5.2 *Creating Internal Links (Hyperlinks)*

An internal link is a link to a topic within the same online help.

1. Switch to the **Content Explorer**.

2. Double-click on the topic in which the internal link needs to be placed.

3. Highlight the text or image (icon) in the topic that is to be used for creating a link.

4. Select from the **Insert** menu the **Hyperlink** command. The dialog box **Insert Hyperlink** opens.

5. Select in the section **Link to** the source type for the target anchor and then select on the right the desired source.

6. The other controls in the dialog box specify the link behavior:

   - The field **Link Text** contains the text that was selected in the topic for the source anchor. When the text is changed here it will also be changed in the topic.

   - **Target Frame** allows for selecting if the destination topic is displayed in the same or in a different window.

   - Enter explanatory text (tool tip) into **Screen Tip**.

   - Select in **Style Class** a style of type a.<styleclass> that is used for formatting the link. Flare will use the basic A tag style when no style is selected.

7. Click **OK** to accept the settings. The dialog box closes and the link is inserted into the topic.

8. Save the topic by opening the **File** menu and selecting the **Save** command.

6.6.5.3 *Creating External Links (Hyperlinks)*

An external link is a link to a topic in a different online help. The online help can ultimately be stored in the same or in a different folder. Therefore, the path specifications always have to be relative to the source topic.

The following information is necessary before an external link can be created:

- name of the external help

- name of the topic in the external help

- for the case that the online help is stored in a different folder: the path to the external help

Follow these steps to create a link to a topic in an external online help:

1. Switch to the **Content Explorer**.

2. Double-click on the topic in which the external link needs to be placed.

3. Highlight the text in the source topic that is to be used for creating a link (hotspot).

4. Select from the **Insert** menu the **Hyperlink** command. The dialog box **Insert Hyperlink** opens.

5. Select in the section **Link to** the option **External Topic**.

6. Enter the destination topic with the applicable syntax shown below directly into **External Topic** on the right:

   When the external HTMLHelp is in the same folder:

   ```
   <ExternalHelp>.chm::/<topic>htm
   ```

   When the external HTMLHelp is located in a different folder:

   ```
   mk:@MSITStore:<PathToExternalHelp>\
   <ExternalHelp>.chm::/<topic>htm
   ```

   When the external online help is WebHelp (Plus) or DotNctHelp enter "../" for every folder that is one level up, for example:

   ```
   ../../<PathToExternalHelp>/<NameOfExternalHelp>/Content/
   <PathToTopic>/<topic>.htm
   ```

7. Specify the link behavior with the other controls in the dialog box.

8. Click **OK** to accept the settings. The dialog box closes and Flare creates the link in the topic.

9. Save the topic by opening the **File** menu and selecting the **Save** command.

6.6.5.4 *Creating Cross-references*

Cross-references are also internal links and can be used the same way as links. Cross-references have, in comparison to links, the advantage that they can be automated through the stylesheet. The cross-reference style can be defined in such a way so that it, for example, always uses the title of the destination topic as the source anchor.

When building the online help all cross-references are updated. A link is always tied to the text of the source anchor that was selected or entered. Changes to the context for that link always require manual adjustments to the source anchor text.

1. Switch to the **Content Explorer**.

2. Double-click on the topic in which the cross-reference needs to be placed.

3. Highlight the text in the source topic that is to be used for creating a link (hotspot).

4. Select from the **Insert** menu the **Cross-Reference** command. The dialog box **Insert Cross-Reference** opens.

5. Select in the section **Link to** the source type and then choose the applicable source on the right.

6. Select in **Cross-Reference Properties** a style class of type XREF, which is to be used for formatting the link. On the right side in the **XREF Format** section is the current format of the XREF tag shown. The controls allow:

    - using the base XREF tag the way it is

    - using a custom style class that is based on the XREF tag

    - clicking on **Edit** to change the custom or basic XREF tag in the **Edit Cross-Reference Style Class** dialog box

    - clicking on **New** for creating a new XREF style class

7. The other fields in the dialog box are used to further specify the behavior of the links:

    - Target Frame allows setting whether the destination topic is to be displayed in the same or in a different window.

    - Enter explanatory text (tool tip) into the field **Screen Tip**.

8. Click **OK** to accept the settings. The dialog box closes and the link is added to the topic.

9. Save the topic by opening the **File** menu and selecting the **Save** command.

6.6.5.5 *Creating Text Popups*

Text popups show explanations in a special text window similar to tool tips, for example, for technical terms or acronyms.

1. Switch to the **Content Explorer**.

2. Double-click on the topic in which the text popup needs to be placed.

3. Highlight the text in the source topic that is to be used as the source anchor (hotspot).

4. Select from the **Insert** menu the command **Text Popup**. The dialog box **Insert Text Popup** appears. The selected text is automatically entered into **Hotspot Text**.

5. Enter the text to be displayed into **Popup Text**.

6. Click **OK** to accept the settings. The dialog box closes and the text popup is added to the topic.

7. Save the topic by opening the **File** menu and selecting the **Save** command.

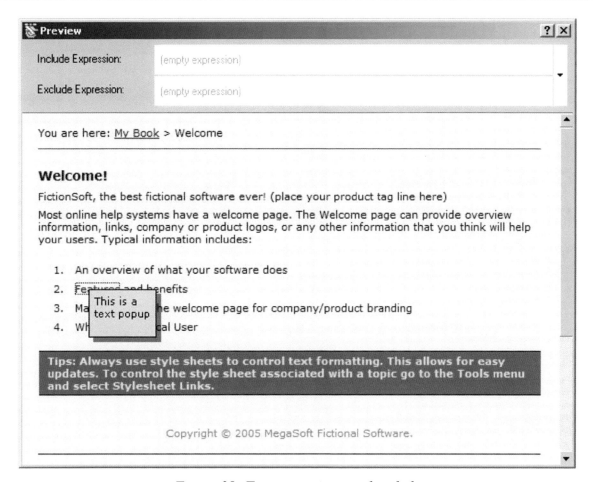

Figure 38: Text popup in an online help

6.6.5.6 Creating Topic Popups

1. Switch to the **Content Explorer**.

2. Double-click on the topic in which the topic popup needs to be placed.

3. Highlight the text in the source topic that is to be used as the source anchor (hotspot).

4. Select from the **Insert** menu the command **Topic Popup**. The dialog box **Insert Topic Popup** appears. The **Target Frame** selection is already set and the text for the source anchor has been automatically entered into **Link Text**.

5. Select in the section **Link to** the source type for the target anchor and then select on the right the desired source.

6. The other controls in the dialog box allow one to further specify the link behavior:

    *   The field **Link Text** contains the previously selected text. Changing the text here will also change the text in the topic.

    *   Enter explanatory text (tool tip) into **Screen Tip**.

    *   The **Style Class** "Popup" is already selected, but the setting can be change to any style class of the type a.<styleclass> for formatting the link.

7. Click **OK** to accept the settings. The dialog box closes and the text popup is added to the topic.

8. Save the topic by opening the **File** menu and selecting the **Save** command.

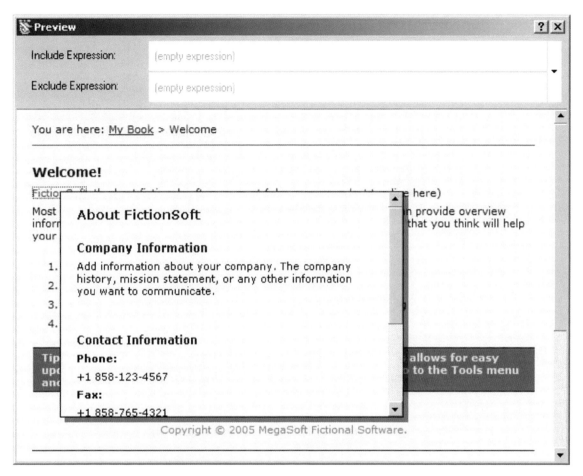

Figure 39: Topic popup in an online help

6.6.5.7 Creating Glossary Term Links

Glossary term links allow for adding new glossary entries during typing and also allow for marking glossary terms in the text.

1. Switch to the **Content Explorer**.

2. Double-click on the topic in which the glossary term link needs to be placed.

3. Highlight the text in the source topic that is to be used as the source anchor (hotspot).

4. Select from the **Insert** menu the command **Glossary Term Link**. When the term

- is already added to the glossary it gets formatted based on the style properties for a glossary term link,

- when the term was not added to a glossary the **Create Glossary Term** dialog box appears. The selected text is already entered in **Term**.

5. Enter the explanation for the glossary term into **Definition**.

6. Choose under **Select Glossary File** the glossary to which the term and definition are to be added.

7. Click **OK** to accept the settings. The style class for glossary term links can be configured in the glossary, see "Editing a Glossary" in section 6.6.3 "Glossary".

8. Save the topic by opening the **File** menu and selecting the **Save** command.

6.6.6 "See Also" Links

"See Also" links present within a topic a collection to related topics. A "See Also" link is displayed as a single link or button. Both open a menu from which the reader can select a topic for further reading. The menu entries are based on the topic title which can be set in the topic properties, see section 4.5.3 "Topic Properties".

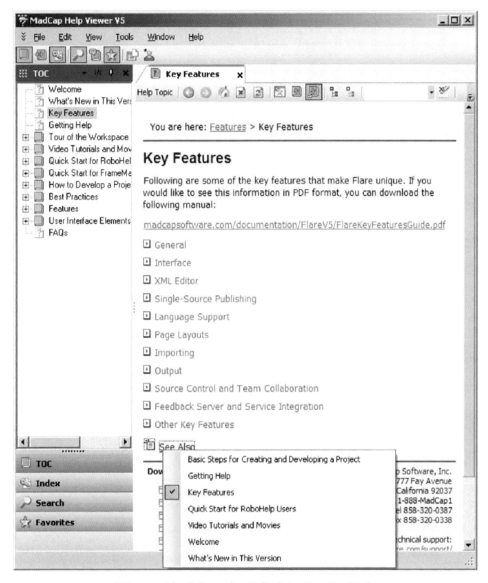

Figure 40: "See Also" link in DotNetHelp

Flare offers three different variations of "See Also" links that do not differ in the way they get displayed in a topic, but in the way they are created and maintained:

- Concept Link: Bundles several topics with a concept marker in a concept. Flare updates the concept links automatically when the marker is deleted from the topic or the marker is inserted into additional topics.

- Keyword Link: Bundles several topics based on a common keyword. Flare updates the links automatically when deleting the keyword from a topic or inserting the keyword in additional topics.

- Related Topic: Bundles singular links without any commonalities. These "Related Topics" links are created more quickly, but are also more difficult to maintain because they have to be updated manually.

6.6.6.1 Concept Link

A concept link bundles several topics of a concept. A project can contain as many concepts as desired. Topics are associated with a concept through a concept marker. All topics with the same concept marker are bundled in a concept link. Flare updates the concept links automatically when the marker is deleted from the topic or the marker is inserted into additional topics.

For establishing concept links, each topic that is to be associated with the concept needs a concept marker inserted. After that, a concept link is inserted into all the topics that are associated with the concept.

Specifying a Concept

1. Change to the **Content Explorer**.

2. Open the topic that is to be associated with a concept via double-click.

3. Select from the **Tools** menu the entry **Concept** and choose from there the **Concept Entry Window** command. The **Concept Entry** window opens on the right side of the workspace.

4. Place the cursor at the beginning of the topic.

5. Enter the name of the concept into the **Concept Entry** editor and press the enter key. A concept marker is added in the topic at the current cursor position.

6. Repeat these steps for all topics associated with a concept.

Inserting a Concept "See Also" Link

1. Open the topic that is to be associated with a concept via double-click.

2. Place the cursor at a suitable position in the topic, for example in the last line.

3. Select from the **Insert** menu the command **Help Control** and from the sub-menu the command **Concept Link**. The dialog box **Insert Concept Link Control** appears.

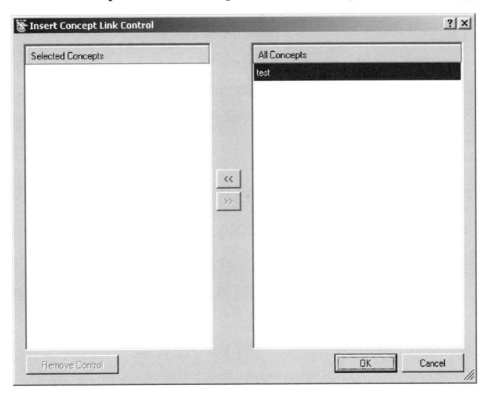

Figure 41: Insert Concept Link Control

4. Select from the list **All Concepts** the desired concept.

5. Click on << to move the desired concept into the list **Selected Concepts**.

6. Click **OK** to accept the settings. The dialog box closes and inserts the "See Also" link at the current cursor position in the topic.

7. Save the topic by opening the **File** menu and selecting the **Save** command.

8. Repeat these steps for all topics that are associated with the concept.

6.6.6.2 *Keyword Link*

A keyword link bundles topics based on a common keyword. A project can contain as many keywords as desired. All topics with the same keyword are bundled into a link when building the output. Flare updates the links automatically when deleting the keyword from a topic or inserting the keyword in additional topics.

The same keyword needs to be entered into all topics that are to be bundled before the link can be created, see "Adding an Individual Index Entry" in section 6.6.2 "Index". After that, a "See Also" link is inserted into all topics of the bundle.

Inserting a Keyword Link

1. Open the topic that is to be associated with a concept via double-click.

2. Place the cursor at a suitable position in the topic, for example, in the last line.

3. Select from the **Insert** menu the command **Help Control** and from the sub-menu the command **Keyword Link Control**. The dialog box **Insert Keyword Link Control** opens.

4. Select from the list **All Keywords** the desired keyword.

5. Click on << to move the selected keyword into the list **Selected Keywords**.

6. Click on **OK** to accept the selection. The dialog box closes and Flare inserts a "Search Index" link at the current cursor position in the topic.

7. Save the topic by opening the **File** menu and selecting the **Save** command.

8. Repeat these steps for all topics that are associated with the keyword.

6.6.6.3 Related Topics

A "Related Topics" link bundles singular links without any commonalities. These "Related Topics" links are created more quickly, but are also more difficult to maintain because they have to be updated manually.

1. Open the topic that is to be associated with a concept via double-click.

2. Place the cursor at a suitable position in the topic, for example, in the last line.

3. Select from the **Insert** menu the command **Help Control** and from the sub-menu the command **Related Topics Control**. The dialog box **Insert Related Topics Control** opens.

4. Select from the list **Folders** the folder with the applicable topic that the link is supposed to reference.

5. Select from the list **Files** the topic that is to be added to the "Related Topics" link and click << to add it to the list.

6. Repeat the steps 4 and 5 until all desired topics are added.

7. Click **OK** to accept the settings. The dialog box closes and Flare inserts a "Related Topics" link at the current cursor position in the topic.

8. Save the topic by opening the **File** menu and selecting the **Save** command.

6.6.6.4 Relationship Tables

Relationship tables are the typical means of referencing topics in DITA document sets. Before the relationships can be displayed in the documentation, the topics of the various topic classes have to be mapped in a relationship table (see section 4.3 "Topic Classes").

A relationship table is built like this:

Table 14: Structure of a Relationship Table

Concept	Task	Reference
Topic X	Topic Y	Topic Z1
		Topic Z2

By default, topic X contains links to topics Y, Z1, and Z2. Topic Y links to topics X, Z1, and Z2. Topics Z1 and Z2 each link to topics X and Y, but not to each other. How the links are presented and in which way they link can be set through the collection type and the linking behavior for each cell.

The available collection types or groupings are:

- unordered (default): the links are displayed in no particular order
- family: links will be created not only to the other topics in the row, but also to all topics in the current cell
- sequence: the links are ordered in the output based on significance
- choice: allows specifying which links are supposed to get "selected" or "highlighted" within the group of links
- use CONREF target (only for DITA output): this link uses the CONREF attribute to pull in content for reuse

The available linking behaviors are:

- normal (default): the link works in all directions and will be displayed in each topic involved
- source only: the topic specified in the cell will have a link to all the other related topics, but all other related topics will not link back to this topic
- target only: the topic specified in the cell with not have a link, but all other related topics will link to this topic

- use CONREF target (only for DITA output): this link uses the CONREF attribute to pull in content for reuse

An in-depth description about collection types and linking behavior can be found in the online resources provided by OASIS (http://xml.coverpages.org/dita.html).

Adding a Relationship Table

Follow these steps to add a relationship table to a project:

1. Select from the **Project** menu the command **Advanced** and from the sub-menu the command **Add Relationship Table...** .The dialog box **Add Relationship Table** appears.

2. Select a different **Template** for the new relationship table if desired.

3. Enter a **File Name** for the new relationship table.

4. Accept the settings by clicking on **Add**. The dialog box closes and a confirmation message appears indicating that the new relationship table file is copied to the specified destination.

5. Proceed by clicking on **OK**. The dialog box closes, the new relationship table (file extension .flrtb) is added to the folder **Advanced** in the **Project Organizer**. The new relationship table is opened in the editor for editing. The table has four columns. The **Row Name** column is for the key words used for identifying the relationships. The columns **concept**, **task,** and **reference** indicate the topic classes and are used for specifying the topics for a relationship.

6. Right-click on a table row and select **Row Properties** from the context menu. The **Row Properties** dialog box appears.

7. Enter a name in **Row Type** and click **OK**. The **Row Properties** dialog box closes and the entry appears in the **Row Name** cell. The row type can be selected from the **Row Type** drop-down list when it is needed for other relationships of the same type.

8. Click into a **concept**, **task**, or **reference** cell of the current row and click ▦. The **Open File** dialog box appears.

9. Select the desired topic and click **Open**. The **Open File** dialog box closes and the topic is inserted into the selected cell.

10. If desired, select a cell with a link and right-click to select the **Cell Properties** command from the context menu. Set **Collection Type** as well as **Linking** to the applicable values. Click **OK** to close the **Cell Properties** dialog box. When a collection type other than the default is selected, the cell will be shaded in green, for a non-default linking behavior the shading will be blue.

11. Click ▦ to add a new row to the table. Perform the same steps as before to fill in the topics for the relationship. It is possible to delete rows as well as columns and also to add new, custom columns when needed.

12. Select from the **File** menu the command **Save** to save the changes in the relationship table.

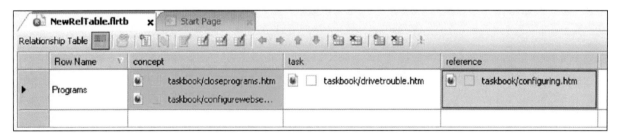

Figure 42: Relationship table in Flare

Inserting a Relationships Proxy

When Flare imports a DITA document set a master page is created that already contains a relationships proxy. The contents of the proxy are determined by a relationship table. The concept of relationship tables and proxies may be useful for other outputs besides DITA. In which case the relationships proxy needs to be added to a master page or directly to the topics that are connected through relationships. The relationships proxy will not display any content when the topic is not mapped to a relationship in a relationship table (see "Proxies" in section 5.7.1 "Master Pages").

Follow these steps to add a relationships proxy:

1. Open the topic or master page that needs a relationships proxy.

2. Place the cursor at the position where the proxy is to be added. Typically, this is at the end of a topic or below the body proxy on a master page.

3. Select from the **Insert** menu the command **Proxy** and from the sub-menu the command **Insert Relationships Proxy...**. The **Relationships Proxy** dialog box appears.

4. Select a stylesheet class for the proxy from the drop-down list or leave it blank to use the default styles. After clicking **OK** the dialog box closes and the relationships proxy is inserted at the current cursor position.

5. Select from the **File** menu the command **Save** to save the changes in the topic or master page.

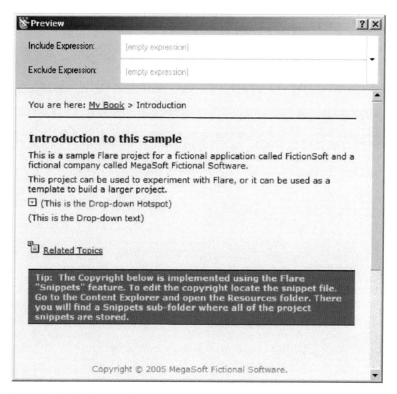

Figure 43: Relationships proxy at the end of a topic in preview

6.6.7 Sensitive Elements

Sensitive elements allow layering of information in a topic. This information is in the topic, but not immediately visible. Readers can display the additional information by clicking on the sensitive element.

6.6.7.1 Adding Expanding Text

1. Change to the **Content Explorer**.

2. Open the topic that needs the expanding text added.

3. Highlight the text in the topic that is to be used as a sensitive element (hotspot).

4. Select from the **Insert** menu the command **Expanding Text**. The **Insert Expanding Text** dialog box appears. The selected text is placed into the hotspot text box automatically.

5. Click **OK** to add the expanding text. The dialog box closes and two pairs of square brackets are inserted at the place of the selected text. The first pair of square brackets contains the selected text and a "|T|" symbol for the hotspot:

Click Me: ▯ ▯ ▯

6. Enter into the second pair of square brackets the text that is supposed to be displayed after clicking the sensitive element. Make sure not to delete any of the brackets.

7. The text inside the square brackets can be edited at any time.

8. Save the topic by opening the **File** menu and selecting the **Save** command.

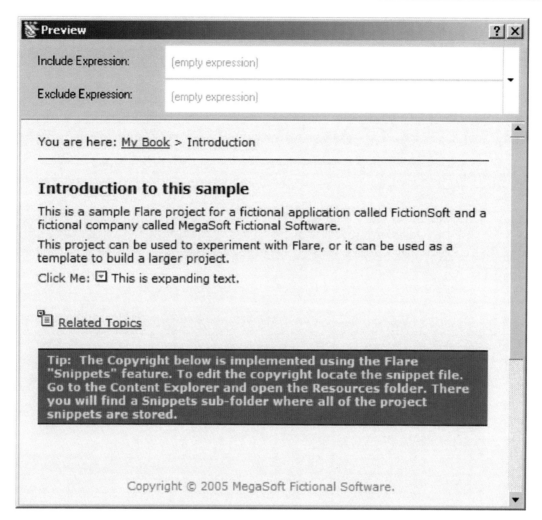

Figure 44: Example for expanding text

6.6.7.2 Adding Drop-down Text

1. Change to the **Content Explorer**.

2. Open the topic that needs the expanding text added.

3. Highlight the text in the topic that is to be used as a sensitive element (hotspot).

4. Select from the **Insert** menu the command **Drop-Down Text**. The dialog box **Insert Drop-Down** appears. The selected text is automatically placed into the **Drop-Down Head** text box.

5. Click **OK** to insert the drop-down text. The dialog box closes and a pair of square brackets and a pair of parentheses are inserted below each other into the topic at the place of the selected text. The square brackets contain the text for the hotspot (head) and the parentheses contain the text for the drop-down (body).

   ⊡ [(This.is.the.Drop-down.Hotspot)]
   (This.is.the.Drop-down.text)

6. Enter the drop-down text replacing the sample text and the parentheses.

7. The text can be edited at any time. It is further possible to insert pictures, tables, or additional sensitive elements.

8. Save the topic by opening the **File** menu and selecting the **Save** command.

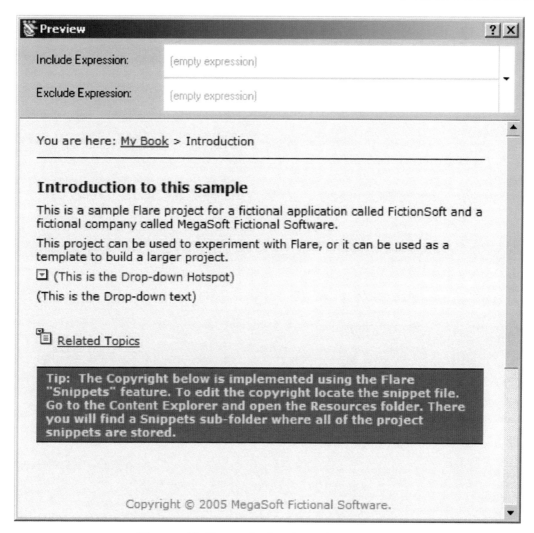

Figure 45: Example for drop-down text

6.6.7.3 Adding an Image Map

1. Change to the **Content Explorer**.

2. Open the topic that needs the image map added.

3. Insert the picture for the image map by expanding the **Insert** menu and selecting the **Picture** command.

4. Right-click on the picture in the topic and select the **Image Map** command from the context menu. The **Image Map Editor** appears showing the selected picture.

5. Select a shape symbol in the **Image Map Editor,** for example, a rectangle.

6. Click and hold the mouse button while dragging the rectangle shape so that it covers that area in the picture that is to be used for a link. After releasing the mouse button, the rectangle has a red frame and is selected. A selected shape can be edited or deleted.

7. Select from the **Edit** menu the **Properties** command. The **Properties** dialog box opens.

8. Select from **Link to** the link type for the destination anchor and then select on the right the destination for the link.

9. The other controls in the dialog box allow one to further specify the behavior of the link:

    -   Select from **Target Frame** if the destination is to be displayed in the same or in a different window.

    -   Enter explanatory text (tool tip) into the **Screen Tip** text box.

10. Click **OK** to accept the settings. The dialog box closes and the link is added to the image map.

11. Mark other areas in the picture in the same way.

12. Select from the **File** menu the **OK** command to save the image map. The **Image Map Editor** closes.

13. Save the topic by opening the **File** menu and selecting the **Save** command.

6.6.8   Interactive Element (only for HTML Help)

Before one can add an interactive element (shortcut) the following information needs to be obtained from the software developers:

- path to the executable file

- parameters that may be expected from the application

- a message ID

- values for the W and L parameters

Interactive elements only work in HTMLHelp that is

- displayed in a help window

- stored on a local drive

For adding an interactive element follow these steps:

1. Change to the **Content Explorer**.

2. Open the topic that needs the interactive element added.

3. Place the cursor at the position in the topic where the interactive elements is supposed to be located.

4. Select from the **Insert** menu the **Help Control** entry and choose the **Shortcut Control** command. The **Insert Shortcut Control** dialog box opens.

5. Enter the information that the software developers provided.

6. Click **OK** to accept the settings. The dialog box closes and the interactive element is inserted into the topic at the current cursor position.

7. Save the topic by opening the **File** menu and selecting the **Save** command.

7 Accessibility

Accessible design means that people with disabilities can utilize an electronic offering without restrictions and assistance of other people. In regards to usability, an accessible online help has to go beyond basic accessibility: users with disabilities are supposed to make use of the electronic offering with the capabilities that they have. Accessibility is the usability in conjunction with a disability or limitation.

The exact number of users that are affected is difficult to establish. Most studies find that about one fifth of the population has some kind of disability and are likely to have to overcome some barrier when using electronic media.

Barriers exist especially when users

- cannot see well or are blind

- cannot hear well or are deaf

- are limited in movement, for example, cannot make use of a mouse

Additionally, barriers can be based on cognitive limitations, for example, attention disorders. It is not only those with disabilities that may encounter barriers, but also anyone who uses a non-standard computer with non-standard input and output devices.

7.1 Assistive Technology

Someone who cannot see well or is blind most likely has the highest barriers for using electronic media. This is based on the necessity that special technical tools, also called assistive technologies, have to be used.

Alternative Output

Blind people and those with other visual impairments need to use software that collects the signals going to the monitor and interpret them anew. One variation is special or bridge software that is called "screen reader". A screen reader either translates the screen contents into synthetic speech, for example, through a sound card, or into signals for a Braille terminal. This is a special output device that reproduces parts of the screen content on a tactile display and is usually combined with a keyboard as input / output device. An audio browser acoustically reproduces content and formatting of a page.

Both tools come with limitations: pictures and symbols still cannot be viewed. Users of screen readers first have to listen to the information before they can determine if it is useful. The more experienced users only have the beginnings of paragraphs or links read to them. The users scan auditorily.

Someone who cannot see also cannot make use of a mouse. Vendors of screen readers have developed some less than ideal solutions. Misunderstandings often occur, for example, a screen reader may read the label of a button, but not instruct the user if the button has to be single or double clicked. Also, a layout that is visually intuitive may be difficult to make usable for the visually impaired.

Modified Output

A screen magnifier shows parts of the "normal" display enlarged on the monitor. This means that the user can only see a small part of the original screen content. When the magnifier is set to scale up fourfold then the user sees only $1/16^{th}$ of the original screen content. This can cause that context gets lost that is necessary for understanding the contents. Many users sit, despite the screen magnifier, very close to the monitor in order to see anything. This leads to a cramped position and is tiring for the eyes.

Other adjustments of the display through changes in the control panel, for example, different settings for colors, can be very helpful for visually impaired persons. These settings also apply to applications – which includes the browser. In some cases this causes problems when designers define custom colors, but leave some color settings up to the system to manage.

Mouse Replacements

Some users cannot make use of a mouse and therefore have to use the keyboard for navigation or for steering the mouse pointer. A template placed on top of the keyboard helps people with limited motor skills to press the correct keys. Also, experts among computer users often prefer the use of the keyboard over a mouse. Working exclusively with the keyboard often allows for working faster.

Keyboard shortcuts for HTML pages are not typically added, but they are possible to be implemented. Having the ability to control a page exclusively through the keyboard is an important aspect for accessibility. People who cannot open their hands often use track balls for navigation, but these often do not allow for exact positioning.

Other Barriers

Most visually handicapped people face barriers even when they don't have to use a screen reader or a magnifier. It is difficult to define requirements for screen display so that it suits these users because there are many forms of visual impairment.

There are many other challenges, such as for people with attention disorders. A logical navigation that is easy to understand can be very helpful. Another example: blinking elements can cause a complete diversion from the content and in some cases even become health hazards.

7.2 Legal Framework

In the United States the laws governing web accessibility are: the Americans with Disabilities Act (ADA), the Individuals with Disabilities Education Act (IDEA), and the Rehabilitation Act of 1973 (specifically section 504 and especially section 508). Individual states and other government bodies may have additional laws and regulations that may apply. While some laws are geared towards federal bodies some laws also apply to private businesses, especially when they operate mainly via the World Wide Web.

The law most commonly referenced is Section 508 of the Rehabilitation Act. In regards to web pages many consider Section 508 compliance as the desired state of accessibility. The parts "Software Applications and Operating Systems (1194.21)" and "Web-based Intranet and Internet Information Applications (1194.22)" of Section 508 are likely the most important parts in regards to online help. The United States Postal Service published in handbook AS-508-A practical guidelines and examples on how to achieve Section 508 compliance and how to test for compliance.

Another generally accepted accessibility standard for the web is defined in the Web Content Accessibility Guidelines. Version 1.0 was released in 1999. The W3C updated the Web Content Accessibility Guidelines in 2004 to a draft of version 2.0, the final version was released in December 2008. The Accessibility Guideline is broken down into four main principles:

- Perceivable
- Operable
- Understandable
- Robust

7.2.1 Perceivable

Users need all contents and functions to be in a form that they can perceive. Especially the orientation of the text as well as suitable contrasts and colors are important. The requirements of this principle assist people with

- visual impairments
- cognitive impairments
- linguistic impairments

Text and hypertext are the only means of displaying information that are supported by all media in the computer world. Text can be processed automatically and presented in all kinds of different forms. Changing text into acoustic output is standard procedure and translating text into other languages is possible with limitations. The connection between text and symbols, pictures, or animations based on text interpretation is also generally possible. An automatic interpretation of graphical information is in comparison much more complicated. Conclusion: many things can be accomplished with text and from text.

Text can be displayed on small screens with low resolutions, which cannot display pictures appropriately. The usage of custom display formats allow for device and user specific display of text and printouts. These benefits are used already by blind or visually impaired people with their terminal equipment.

User specific conditioning (rendering, profiling) allow for providing the texts to other user groups. The conditioning for other user groups is not that vastly developed, but browsers that make use of avatars, pictures, and animations are feasible. On the contrary, information that is not available as text, creates a barrier for people with disabilities. The use of graphical aids is important for many users, which means that a text only display is not a solution.

7.2.2   Operable

This principle refers especially to device independence for input. For example, blind people cannot operate a mouse pointer. Also, people with visual and motor impairments generally prefer using the keyboard. Often enough only parts of a page can be controlled with a keyboard.

The requirements of this principle assist people who

- are blind or visually impaired
- are challenged with the hand-eye coordination required for some input devices
- are physically impaired
- cannot operate pointing devices effectively
- have linguistic or learning disabilities
- make use of voice input

These users often do not notice an unannounced switch of windows. They may not realize they are no longer on a page, but in a popup window. This is a problem for people who are blind, have difficulties with seeing, or who cannot comprehend the automatic switch. Even the display of a link destination in a secondary window leads to confusion for some users. The important browser feature of browsing back appears to no longer work.

Tickers or changing contents dictate the reading speed for users, which some are unable to achieve for various reasons. Flickers or flashes through animations can cause seizures for some people. When these effects are necessary they should be controllable by the user.

Being able to orient oneself on a page or in an online help is important for the effective usage of the   content. A system that cannot be navigated because it is not suitable for the access technology used or that is too confusing or complicated for some users, blocks the way to all other content.

Special browsers allow visually impaired persons to navigate from hyperlink to hyperlink or from heading to heading. Therefore, hyperlinks and headings have to be self-explanatory. Link anchor texts such as "click here", "more", or "Information"; or frame names such as "Frame1" or "Frame2" are useless without any context information. Wrongly leveled headings are very confusing. Also, persons with learning challenges, learning disabilities, or developmental disabilities need a solid navigation framework to find their way on a page.

Generally, the direct relationship to the context is important so that the desired information can be found quickly. The aspect of large areas and readability is of importance for people who have mobility problems or visual impairments.

A good and consistent navigation is an important foundation for the general usability of a hypertext. Full text search and navigational mechanisms are supposed to help orient oneself. A targeted search through a clear and meaningful navigation is helpful. Meaningful labeling of navigational elements and hyperlinks, comprehensible structuring, information about the current position in a document, return links to the main categories, and so forth are common practice in many well-designed sites.

7.2.3   Understandable

Comprehensibility improves the general usability. A simple language suitable for the content enhances the comprehensibility of the documents. Documents with a clear structure are easier to understand. Graphics, pictures, and audio clips help users to grasp the content much easier.

Acronyms and technical terms are common in today's language. An explanation at the point of use helps readers. Thus, documents are easier to understand for users of any educational level, for those who are not native speakers, or when readers are tired or distracted.

Active efforts for enhancing comprehensibility are especially important for people who use sign language. Simple language, media elements, symbols, pictures, and so on help people with learning problems or learning disabilities to comprehend the contents easier. People who use voice output can follow along more easily when they don't have to endure long sentences.

In order to improve comprehensibility the learning methods and experiences of users have to be taken into account. Using simple and descriptive language, applicable metaphors, stressing differences and similarities of concepts, and explaining uncommon terms can also help to increase understandability.

7.2.4   Robust

Contents have to be sufficiently robust so that they can work with current and future technologies. This principle is more of a technical nature and points towards the use of available and accessible standards. The use of XHTML for structuring information and Cascading Style Sheets (CSS) for layout and formatting are one aspect, but also technologies such as multimedia need to be implemented following applicable standards so that any access software can work.

The adherence to standards ensures the usability in a complex system and provides:

- a guarantee of compatibility
- a guarantee for developers of new agents and tools
- a guarantee for usability for the users
- the ability to process content and display it accordingly (rendering)

Application islands are created when standards are not applied correctly. These islands can then only be used under special conditions. This happens when, for example, a specific browser with proprietary functions is needed to correctly display the content, if specific additions (plug-ins) are needed, or when a specific screen resolution is necessary.

When tags are used incorrectly agents may interpret the content incorrectly. One problem is special formatting for the representation of a structure or structuring for a special format. This can lead to massive barriers for people with disabilities because the assistive technologies that they use interpret tags in such a way that the presented content has nothing to do with the context.

Users do not use the most current version of browsers or software for various reasons, and often some features are disabled or some plug-ins are missing. The reasons are as various as the number of users. Some are used to the complex functions of a software, while others have spent a lot of effort to personalize settings. These users are less inclined to download and install the newest version.

The latest and greatest also does not necessarily run on older hardware or under any version of an operating system. Maybe the user does not know about an update. Security is another concern when activating plug-ins, scripts, or cookies.

When one is reliant on assistive technology it may also not be possible to just switch software and hardware. Some assistive technologies work best with specific versions of specific browsers. And even if the update for the browser is for free, the applicable updates for the assistive technologies are not always free or readily available. Some users deactivate specific features or do not install plug-ins because they cannot use them anyway.

By ignoring standards, designers and authors take away the opportunity for them to use formal test applications that are very helpful with debugging. For example, the W3C offers a free validation service:

CSS   http://jigsaw.w3.org/css-validator/

XHTML   http://validator.w3.org

7.3   Conclusion for Online Help

The laws apply to the Internet, but some innovative software vendors already aim at barrier-free online help: they prevent the need for special solutions for differently abled people by offering one solution for all users – and that with only a little bit of extra effort.

In times where people live longer and want to stay active longer, persons that are visually impaired or blind want to read online helps on screen well. Blind and deaf people especially depend on very good help functions.

Barrier-free information technology needs to be designed in such a way that everyone can make use of it, so that it supports, for example, the use of alternative input and output devices other than monitor and mouse, low bandwidth access, or situational limitations such as mobile applications. This is rarely the case as Jacob Nielsen shows in studies: in a comparison between blind persons, strongly visually impaired persons, and persons without impairments were the people without impairments

- six times more successful than users that use a screen reader
- four times more successful than users who use a screen magnifier

7.3.1 Layout

Blind people and people with visual impairments cannot recognize colors and font formatting that are used not for accentuation, but for differentiation. People who are color blind or have a red-green visual impairment have problems in these situations. This can be prevented by using, for example, special characters in addition to colors and font formatting.

In order to accommodate necessities of visually impaired persons the following aspects should be kept in mind:

- colors of text and background have set each other apart
- colors of individual characters or elements have to have high contrast
- font sizes have to be defined relatively

Red font on green background is much more difficult to see than yellow font on a blue background, or black on white. This is especially important for the design of buttons or symbols because they cannot be manipulated by the browser. In contrast, browsers can ignore the color setting for texts.

The relative size definition for frames, tables, and text is necessary for a design that suits visually impaired people. These relative settings take lower screen resolutions into account. Font sizes that are set through the browser are only applicable when the source text allows for it. The layout should be tested with a screen magnifier before passing it on to production use. Text fonts especially suffer from the aliasing effect that can negatively impact readability.

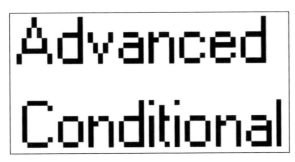

Figure 46: Aliasing with large font

Users of screen magnifiers have to scroll excessively to access all information on a page. The users of screen readers have to capture this information auditorily. Small units of information make it easier for these users to keep the overview, redundant and unnecessary text is an annoyance.

7.3.1.1 Frames

Screen readers can process only one frame at any given point in time. This means that the screen reader has to jump back and forth when a page is split into multiple frames. Frames are generally not a problem anymore for blind or visually impaired people, but frames can still be problematic at times.

Browser based online help systems use the frame technology to display the help window analogous to the Microsoft HTMLHelp viewer. The frames typically have meaningful names such as "Navigation", "Content", and "Toolbar". Ideally the noframe tag is used, for example, with a menu for navigating the page. This would help the blind users with text-only browsers.

7.3.1.2 *Dynamic Effects*

One does not have to do without Java or JavaScript. Although for those cases where interaction is important, alternatives such as a link are necessary. In particular, dynamically generated results are not interpreted correctly by screen readers.

Some screen readers cannot handle Flash based demos and audio sequences drown out the synthetic voice output. For these cases an alternative way of transferring the information is helpful.

Popups and secondary windows should not be used because they are not registered at all or get registered only after several tries. Popups often cover up relevant information that a screen reader cannot detect. The users often only have the option to close the page.

7.3.1.3 *Audio and Video*

Multimedia effects will always be a barrier for a specific group of people. For example, an acoustic signal should therefore always have an optical match and vice versa.

7.3.2 Pictures

The users of screen readers basically cannot view pictures. The only way to find out about the content of the picture is through the alternative text that can be defined for each picture in the HTML source. A screen reader that comes across a picture when interpreting a page will only output "Graphic" and the alternative text.

This is why alternative texts have a high importance for screen readers. A "Please click here" in multiple occurrences is not helpful even for a simple symbol. Alternative texts for pictures have to:

- explain the function of the picture if it is also a link
- describe the picture concisely so that the user can gauge its importance

Many users of screen readers and screen magnifiers turn the display of pictures off, mainly because they came across way too many "useless" pictures. To get a first impression about the accessibility a simple test with a web browser is recommended. The display of pictures can be turned off in the settings of standard browsers. When the pages can still be read without loss of information, then blind and visually impaired persons can use them as well.

Some blind users use the line based Lynx browser, which does not load any pictures, but other browsers are often used as well. In all cases pictures can only be interpreted based on the alternative text. One can quickly determine if navigating a page is difficult or impossible when this alternative text is missing or not meaningful enough.

In addition to the barrier posed by pictures, image maps can only be operated with a mouse. The screen reader detects the picture as such, but cannot interpret the sensitive areas as such. This means image maps are insurmountable barriers for persons who use a screen reader. Linking a picture with a descriptive page is much more elegant and allows for using a picture in a different size.

Visually impaired people need pictures with high-contrast colors. Text in pictures such as callouts or numbers have to be shown in a suitable size.

7.3.3 Tables

As with frames, screen readers can always only process one table row at a time. A meaningful and systematic arrangement of the cell contents makes reading much easier. Tables are structured well for a screen reader when the table rows can be read row by row from left to right.

Tables should not be used for structuring the page layout. Visually impaired and blind users expect structured information in a table and cannot benefit from the tabular layout. Tables should furthermore not be too large and have a short description in the summary property of the table in the HTML source text.

7.3.4 Links

When users of screen readers or screen magnifiers know that a page has many links they will follow the first link that somewhat fits the information that they are looking for. The fewer links a page has the more likely it is that users will find the correct link.

Links should always be underlined and thus follow the de-facto web standard. When users zoom into a screen section multiple times with a screen magnifier they cannot see a more subtle markup for a link such as bold or blue font.

Large buttons and large text for links make it easier for people with impaired motor skills to use them. A lot of white space around these links makes it more likely that these people will click on the desired link and not on the link that precedes or follows.

7.4 *Implementation with Flare*

Flare strictly separates content and layout through XHTML and stylesheets and thus provides good conditions for creating accessible online helps. Stylesheets provide through the parameter medium the option to support not only print and online output, but also other output devices. A selection is shown in the table below.

Table 15: Medium selection in stylesheets

Medium	Meaning
aural	Voice oriented output devices, for example, screen readers
braille	Braille capable output devices
embossed	Braille capable printers
handheld	Output devices with small displays, such as PDAs
projection	Video beamers
screen	Monitors
tty	Output devices with fixed fonts, for example, terminals or mobile phones
tv	Televisions

One example is the optimization for voice output. The same way that regular text can be styled with colors, font types, and font size it can be styled for voice browsers. This can be achieved by using different voices or accentuation mechanisms.

A new medium can be added to the stylesheet and the paragraph formats can be styled for voice output. The online help can then be generated for voice browsers through a new target, see section 5.7.4 "How Everything Comes Together: The Target".

7.4.1   Adding a New Medium for Stylesheets

1. Switch to the **Content Explorer**.

2. Open the folder **Resources \ Stylesheets**.

3. Open the stylesheet via double-click.

4. Select **Advanced View** if not already enabled.

5. Select in the local toolbar of the Stylesheet Editor from the **Options** menu the **Add Medium** command.

6. Enter a name for the new medium, for example, "aural".

7. Click **OK** to accept the entry. The dialog box closes and a new medium is created. The new medium is added to the **Medium** drop-down list.

8. Select the new medium from the drop-down list.

9. Select as display option of the properties the option **Show: Property Groups**.

7.4.2   Voices

The property group **Unclassified** has several properties for specifying the reading voice. Some of these are:

pitch	tone of the voice
pitch-range	tone range of the voice

richness	brightness of the voice
speech-rate	reading speed of the voice
stress	inflection of the voice
voice-family	type of voice, such as female, male, or child

In order to enhance the text for the listener one can, for example, use these properties to create two different voices, such as:

headings (H1, H2, etc.)	voice-family: female
	richness: 35
	pitch: medium
	speech-rate: medium
regular text (P, UL, OL, etc.)	voice-family: male
	richness: 75
	pitch: low
	speech-rate: slow
markup (font style)	stress: 75
	speak: spell-out

It is often beneficial to create speech definitions for only specific words or word groups. In these cases the speak property defines that all letters are to be spoken individually. This is used to articulate an acronym or a technical term in comparison to regular text.

Pauses

Aside from different voices, spoken text also needs pauses and different reading speeds. The property group Unclassified has for this the following properties:

pause	pause definition
pause-after	pause after an element
pause-before	pause before an element
speech-rate	reading speed

The values for the pause properties should not be set too high, because this disturbs the stream of speech unnecessarily. Pauses are recommended for lists, paragraphs, or headings, for example:

headings (H1, H2, etc.)	pause-before: 1500 ms
	pause-after: 1000 ms
regular text (P, UL, OL, etc.)	pause-before: 500 ms
	pause-after: 500 ms
markup (font style)	pause: 500 ms
	speak: spell-out

Special Voice Settings

For some elements – such as tables – it is recommended to change the regular text flow a bit so that the listener can follow the context easier. Tables have a special property for that purpose that defines how tables are read: the speak-header property, which is also found in the **Unclassified** property group.

The speak-header property defines when and how often the column headers are read. The values "once" and "always" specify if the header is read before each row or only once for each column. Depending on the size of the table, one or the other option is more suitable, for example:

Food	Price	Amount
Bread	$2.50	1
Milk	$3.50	3

When the table property **speak-header** is set to **always** the table is spoken as follows:

Food: Bread, Price: $2.50

Food: Bread, Amount: 1

Food: Milk, Price: $3.50

Food: Milk, Amount: 3

When the table property **speak-header** is set to **once** the table is spoken as follows:

Food: Bread, Price: $2.50, Amount: 1

Food: Milk, Price: $3.50, Amount: 3

8 Context Sensitive Connectivity

Users expect a context sensitive help as soon as a software provides a graphical user interface. The context sensitive help is part of the software and is often managed through the software. The context sensitive help provides the reader with information about the element of the graphical user interface for which the help was activated. An online help can be connected context sensitively to various control elements of the user interface:

Table 16: Options of context sensitive connectivity

Control Element	Call	Display
Dialog box	Help button, F1 key, question mark symbol	Online help
Field, command, button, menu, toolbar	F1 key, question mark symbol	Online help
	Hover over with mouse pointer	Tool tip, status bar

The context sensitive help at element level can only provide very selective and isolated information because it focuses only on the specific element. Not every element in the graphical user interface has to be connected to context sensitive help. Users become unhappy when the context sensitive help contains irrelevant information. Most of the time it makes more sense to bundle options and point to the differences in the description. The descriptions should be clear and brief.

Context sensitive help at the dialog box level describes a dialog box, a window, or an entire tab including all elements. The help describes each user interface element as well as the relationship between the elements.

Usability tests showed that users cannot always detect that the information already fits the context because the help window looked the same as when accessing context free help. The help window should come up without any navigation to make it easier for the users to identify context sensitive help.

8.1   Zipper Mode

The connection between software and help works like a zipper. One side of the zipper is the element in the user interface, the other side is the topic that describes the element. Either two control files or the URL of the topic act as the zipper depending on the development environment and for which target system the interface was developed. The control files are the so called header file and alias file.

8.1.1   Header File

The header file is a flat text file in which each element of the user interface has an identifier and a context number assigned. The context number is also called map ID. Most development environments can create the header file with the click of a button, but Flare can generate a header file as well. The header file has to be coordinated between the technical writer and the graphical user interface (GUI) developer, and it needs to be kept current.

The header file has the following structure:

```
#define <identifier> <map ID>
```

The separator between the three components is a space. The identifier or the map ID are not allowed to have spaces. Each identifier and map ID can only be used once within a project, they have to be unique.

Examples:

```
#define welcome 1
#define new_project_dialog_box 2
#define NewFileDialogBox 3
```

A naming convention for the identifiers is recommended for complex projects. This way, different writers can easily figure out which element the identifier references. The help compiler does not make a difference between upper and lower case. Most special characters are allowed.

The header file in a Flare project is found in the **Project Organizer** in the folder **Advanced**.

8.1.2   Alias File

The alias file is the real zipper that maps identifiers with topics. The alias file also allows connecting the context sensitive topics with a skin, which suppresses the navigation. The alias file in a Flare project is found in the **Project Organizer** in the folder **Advanced** and has the file extension .flali.

8.1.3   URL

The URL defines the position of a topic in an online help. The URL for a topic of a Flare project is comprised of the path and the topic name in the following format:

```
<helpname>/Contents/<pathtotopic>/<topicname>.htm
```

Depending on how the help is integrated into the application the name of the online help as well as the topic name may be sufficient.

8.2   Shared Tasks

The context sensitive help can only be realized through the cooperation between the technical writer and the GUI developer. In one or more rounds of decision making the following points have to be agreed upon:

- type of context sensitive connection (element level, dialog box level, messages)
- elements that will be connected (overview with names and calls in a table or list)
- help format
- type of help calls (control files, JavaScript, or URL)
- type of help (separate help for context sensitive content or everything in one help)
- necessary information and its exchange (header file, identifiers, map IDs, topic names and paths, etc.)

8.2.1   Tasks of the Technical Writer

Depending on the decisions made with the GUI developer a technical writer may face the following tasks aside from creating content:

- list all GUI elements that are to be included in the context sensitive help
- define URLs or identifiers and map IDs for each GUI element
- read in or create header file or matrix with URLs
- create alias file
- assign an alias to each topic
- generate help
- test help

8.2.2   Tasks of the GUI Developer

Depending on the decisions made with the technical writer a GUI developer may face the following tasks:

- list all GUI elements that are to be included in the context sensitive help
- specify the help properties and help calls for each GUI element
- read in or create header file
- test context sensitive connectivity

8.3   *Implementation with Flare*

Flare can create and export header files as well as import existing header files. The header file is managed by Flare as a text file that can be changed in any way desired. Flare provides concrete support for the following development environments:

- C/C++ (file name extension for header file: .h or .hh)

- Visual Basic (file name extension for header file: .bas)

- Java (file name extension for header file: .properties)

- Delphi (file name extension for header file: .inc)

8.3.1 Creating a Header File

The technical writer needs to create the header file when it has been decided that this is the task of the technical writer.

1. Select from the **Project** menu the entry **Advanced** and in there the **Add Header File** command. The **Add Header File** dialog box opens.

2. Select a template from **Templates** if desired.

3. Enter a name for the header file into **File Name**.

4. Click **Add** and a confirmation message appears asking if the header file is to be created from the selected template.

5. Click **OK** in the confirmation message and the message and the dialog box close. The new header file is created in the **Project Organizer** in the folder **Advanced**.

Editing a Header File

The header file is a flat text file that can be edited in any way desired. The header file can be edited through the text editor of Flare or implicitly through the alias file.

1. Switch to the **Project Organizer**.

2. Open the folder **Advanced**.

3. Open the desired header file via double-click.

4. Add new identifiers.

5. Save the header file by opening the **File** menu and selecting the **Save** command.

Exporting a Header File

In order to pass on the header file to the development team the file needs to be exported for the applicable development environment.

1. Switch to the **Project Organizer**.

2. Open the folder **Advanced**.

3. Right-click on the applicable header file and select the **Export Header File(s)** command from the context menu. The **Export Header Files** dialog box opens.

4. Select the development environment for which the header file is to be exported.

5. Select all header files that are to be exported.

6. Select the export folder for the header files.

7. Click **Export** and the selected header files are exported into the specified folder.

8. Answer the question if the folder should be opened.

Importing a Header File

When the development team creates and maintains the header files then Flare can import them.

1. Select from the **Project** menu the entry **Advanced** and in there the **Add Header File** command. The **Add Header File** dialog box opens.

2. Select a template from **Templates** if desired.

3. Select in **Source File** the path and the header file for import.

4. Enter a new name for the header file in **File Name** if desired.

5. Click **Add** and a message appears asking if the header file is to be copied into the Flare project.

6. Click **OK** and the message and dialog boxes close. The imported header file is now located in the **Project Organizer** in the **Advanced** folder.

8.3.2 Creating an Alias File

The creation and maintenance of the alias file is independent from who is in charge of maintaining the header file. For the context sensitive connection via control files, an alias file is always needed. The alias files link the elements of the graphical user interface to the applicable help topics.

1. Select from the **Project** menu **Advanced** and in there the **Add Alias File** command.

2. Select a template from **Templates** if desired.

3. Enter a name for the alias file in **File Name**.

4. Click **Add** and a message appears asking if the new alias file is to be created from the selected template.

5. Accept the selection by clicking **OK** and the message and dialog box close. The new alias file is created in the **Project Organizer** in the **Advanced** folder and opened for editing.

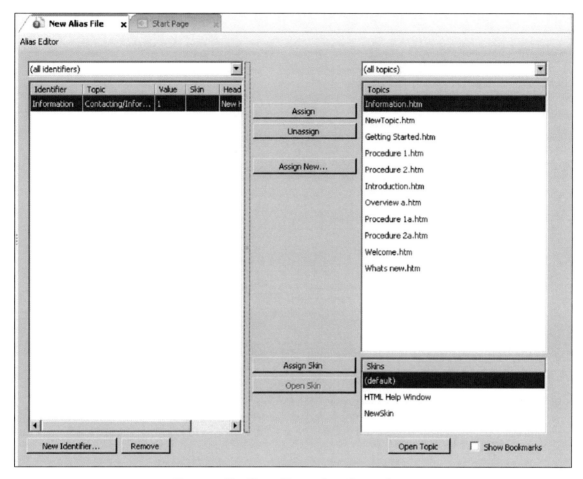

Figure 47: Alias file in the alias editor

Assigning Aliases to Individual Topics

The identifiers in the alias file are used to connect the elements of the graphical user interface with the help topics. The alias file uses the header file of the Flare project. The alias file editor is configured in a way that the identifiers of all header files are shown. A specific header file can be selected from the drop-down list on the left side so that only the identifiers from that header file are shown.

The table on the left shows all identifiers of the selected header file, the table on the right shows all topics in the project. As soon as the assignment of the identifiers to the elements of the graphical user interface is completed, the identifiers can be assigned to the topics.

1. For assigning an identifier to a topic, select the identifier in the table on the left.

2. Select the applicable topic from the list on the right.

3. Click **Assign** to assign the topic to the identifier. The file name of the topic is added to the identifier table.

4. Optionally assign a skin by selecting the desired skin from **Skins** and clicking **Assign Skin**, for example, when the context sensitive topics are to be displayed in a help window without navigation. The skin is also added to the current row identifier table.

5. Repeat the steps 1 through 4 for all context sensitive topics.

6. Save the alias file by opening the **File** menu and selecting the **Save** command.

Adding a New Identifier to the Alias File

The alias editor also allows adding new identifiers and thus editing the header file implicitly.

1. Switch to the **Project Organizer**.

2. Open the folder **Advanced**.

3. Open the applicable alias file via double-click.

4. Click **New Identifier**, which is located below the identifier table. Flare adds a new row into the identifier table and adds **NEW1** as the default name for the new identifier.

5. Click into the first cell of the new row, the cell is now in edit mode and the identifier can be changed.

6. Change the entry based on the requirements.

7. Assign the new identifier to a topic.

8. Add more identifiers to the alias file if needed.

9. Save the alias file by opening the **File** menu and selecting the **Save** command.

Assigning an Alias File

The alias file has to be assigned to the target so that the correct identifiers are added to the output.

1. Switch to the **Project Organizer**.

2. Open the folder **Targets** and open the applicable target via double-click. The target opens.

3. Select the **Advanced** tab and choose from the **Alias File** drop-down list the alias file that is to be used for building.

4. Save the target by opening the **File** menu and selecting the **Save** command.

8.3.3 Building Online Help

To build online help perform the following steps:

1. Switch to the **Project Organizer**.

2. Open the folder **Targets**.

3. Right-click on the desired target and select the **Build** command from the context menu. The help is built and the output is stored in the specified output folder.

Errors during the build process can be stored in a log file. The log file is stored with date and time in the **Project Organizer** in the folder **Reports**. Open the log file via double-click. Double-clicking a listed topic opens the topic for editing.

8.3.3.1 *Testing Context Sensitive Connection*

When testing the context sensitive connection two aspects have to be kept in mind:

- correct assignment of identifiers to topics

- correct assignment of identifiers to the GUI elements

The first aspect can be tested with the help of Flare, the second aspect needs to be tested during the system test or by the GUI developer.

1. Switch to the **Project Organizer**.

2. Open the folder **Targets**.

3. Right-click on the applicable target and select **Test CSI API Calls** from the context menu. The **Context Sensitive Help (CSH) API Tester** dialog box opens. The list shows all identifiers of the header files and the identifier assignments that Flare found in the alias file.

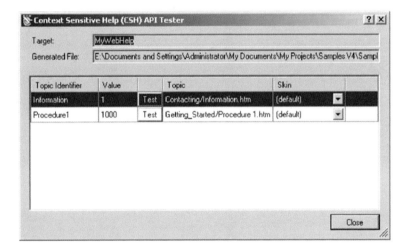

4. Select a skin if desired.

5. Click **Test** for each identifier. The assigned topic opens. If

- the correct topic opens, everything works as desired.

- the wrong topic opens, change the assignment in the alias file.

- no topic opens, the assignment is missing.

9 Multilingualism

In a time of globalization, multilingualism is an important and interesting aspect for online help systems. With the rise of Eastern European and Asian markets, technical writers have to deal with foreign languages and character sets that are unusual for them.

9.1 Unicode

Unicode is an international standard that is intended to consolidate all text characters in worldwide use – letters, numbers, punctuation marks, syllable characters, special characters, and ideograms – into a single alphanumerical character set. Unicode was developed by the International Organization for Standardization (ISO) and the Unicode consortium. Unicode allows displaying multiple languages in the same text.

Unicode contains the letters of the Latin alphabet with all country specific special characters, the Greek, Cyrillic, Arabic, Hebrew, and Thai alphabets as well as the CJK characters – the different Chinese, Japanese, and Korean alphabets. Unicode is therefore independent from languages and character sets and supports internationalization. Unicode further allows localizing applications without code changes with settings for country specific properties and the normalization for diacritic characters. Additionally, special characters for mathematics, business, and technology are coded.

Instead of the ISO defined identification UCS-2, the identifier UTF-16 (UCS Transformation Format 16 bit) is more commonly used, a standard defined by the Unicode consortium. UTF-8 (UCS Transformation Format 8 bit) is also in common use besides UTF-16.

UTF-8 is by now the international character code of the Internet. The Internet Engineering Task Force mandates from all Internet communication protocols that the character code is declared and that UTF-8 is one of the supported codes. UTF-8 displays every Unicode character depending on its position with a length of one to four Bytes. The first 128 characters are identical with ASCII.

Extensive information about Unicode is available from the WWW site of the Unicode consortium: http://www.unicode.org/.

Character Display

Every character in Unicode has a number assigned, the so called code point. A Unicode code point is typically written in the format U+n, where n consists of four to six hexadecimal numbers.

All code points build the code space. The code space of the Unicode standard V4 consists of 1,114,112 code points of which most are not assigned. The code space is separated into levels. Every level consists of 65,536 code points. The most important level is the level 0, the Basic Multilanguage Plain (BMP), which contains the code points from U+0000 to U+FFFF. The code points from U+0000 to U+00FF are identical with those of ISO 8859-1. The code points that are defined in the Unicode standard are listed in code charts. The tables are available from the printed version of the Unicode standard or in the WWW, for example, on the pages of the Unicode consortium.

Unicode and Microsoft Windows

Although ASCII and ANSI are still in popular use on the Windows platform, the NT branch of Windows (Windows NT 4.0, Windows 2000, Windows XP, Windows 2003, Vista, Windows 7) does work internally entirely with Unicode. Almost all functions of the Windows API have two versions. One is used for Unicode and the other for ASCII. This also applies to context sensitive HTMLHelp, which is called through the applicable API.

The function HTMLHelp() actually does not exist. It is only a definition that is mapped to one of the following functions based on the definition of _UNICODE or the lack thereof:

- HtmlHelpA() => ASCII or ANSI version

- HtmlHelpW() => Unicode version ("W" stands for "wide char")

This isn't mentioned explicitly in the Windows API documentation, but it applies to all Windows API functions. The first steps are done for developers to make use of Unicode in context sensitive help connectivity.

Unicode Character Set

Prerequisite for the use of Unicode, and thus for the translation of online helps into Eastern European and Asian languages, are special Unicode fonts. Each font family has a Unicode variant that needs to be installed on the production system. Unicode fonts can be purchased from various vendors.

9.2   *Implementation with Flare*

Flare does not only support Unicode for topic files, but also for all control files of a help project. All files of a help project make use of the UTF-8 code. For example, Lingo can be used for translations of Flare projects. Lingo is a Translation Memory System for Flare projects from Madcap Software.

Lingo allows loading of the source project, translation of all content, and then the exporting of a new Flare project. Lingo provides additional support for the exchange format TMX to connect to other Translation Memory Systems, such as Across or Trados.

When Lingo is not used for the translation of a Flare project, several aspects have to be considered. The main decision is if all language versions are maintained in a single Flare project or if an independent project is created for each language. Both approaches are possible and have advantages and disadvantages.

The one project approach allows for keeping all information for a product in one source. This may lead to growing confusion if the product is complex and several languages have to be supported. Using individual projects prevents confusion and provides a better overview, but it increases the administrative effort.

After deciding on an approach, the scope of translation has to be determined. Potential targets for translations are all those files that contain text that need to be translated, for example, the topics. The technical writer determines which files need to be translated because it is possible that, for example, a master page is designed in such a way that it does not need any translation.

9.2.1 Components for Translations

The following files are potential candidates for translation:

- topics (and with those also tables and index entries)
- table of contents
- glossary
- master page
- pictures
- variables
- snippets
- bookmarks
- skins

All files requiring translation can be passed on as XML files to the translators. Always use the correct language selection when building, for example, for Russian always use Cyrillic (Russia) rather than Cyrillic (Mongolia).

9.2.2 Language Settings in the Flare Project

The language can be set in different places within a Flare project. The settings have a different impact depending on where they are made.

Language of the Project

The language of a project is set when creating a new project, see section 3.6.1 "Creating a Project". This language selection impacts mainly the spell checker. The language can be set at a later point by opening the **Project** menu, selecting the **Project Properties...** command, and setting the desired language on the **Language** tab.

Language of a Topic

Same applies as for the language setting of a project. The language for a topic is set in the properties dialog box, see section 4.5.3 "Topic Properties".

Language of a Skin

The language for the skin of WebHelp and WebHelp Plus projects is set in the target. In the tab **Language** of the target is a language table that contains the column **Localized Skins**, which indicates if a skin is available for the specific target language. The skin needs to be translated as well when no localized skin exists for the selected language.

The language of the skin for HTMLHelp is dependent on the language setting of the production system. This means that Chinese HTMLHelp has to be built on a system with language and regional settings for Chinese. The language and regional settings can be changed in the system administration, which is available, for example, in Windows XP under **Start > Settings > Control Panel > Regional and Language Options**.

9.2.3 Steps for Creating a Project in the Targeted Language

After receiving the translated files the following steps are necessary:

1. Create a new Flare project in the targeted language if needed.

2. Copy (new Flare project) or import (existing Flare project) the translated files into the Flare project.

3. Set the language for the topics if needed.

4. Check and expand the keyword entries in the Index Explorer.

5. Check and expand the table of contents.

6. Build the output and test the result.

7. Change the system language settings if needed and build the output again.

Changing the Keyboard Layout

For small changes to the index or table of contents of the online help the keyboard layout can be set for the target language. The following steps apply to Windows XP:

1. Select in Windows **Start > Settings > Control Panel > Regional and Language Options**. The **Regional and Language Options** dialog box appears.

2. Select the tab **Languages** and click **Details**. The **Text Services and Input Languages** dialog box opens.

3. Click **Add** and the **Add Input Language** dialog box appears.

4. Select from the **Keyboard layout/IME** drop-down list the desired language.

5. Click **OK** to accept the settings. The new selection is added to the list in **Installed services**.

6. Click **OK** to accept the settings. The **Text Services and Input Languages** dialog box closes.

7. Close the **Regional and Language Options** dialog box as well by clicking **OK**. The new keyboard layout is available from the task bar. The symbol in the task bar allows switching between different keyboard layouts so that text in the targeted language can be entered.

Glossary

This glossary explains the technical terms that are used in this book in alphabetical order. The format of the explanations is as follows:

Used Term

Synonyms

> Explanation

Adaptability

Adjustability, convertability

> Users can select the settings such as color or font size based on their personal preferences. Compare to configuration.

API

> Application Programming Interface; programmable interconnection between applications.

Application

System, solution, program, software

> A computer program that is installed on the local computer or accessible through a web browser.

Bar

> Area of a window, such as tool bar or menu bar.

Blooming

> Display problem on monitors, especially cathode ray tube (CRT) monitors. Blooming causes that, for example, black font on a white background appears as thin and fuzzy. The same applies for the opposite (white font on a black background).

Book

Chapter

> Topics that belong together within a help system. This grouping is usually displayed by a book symbol.

Bookmark

Entry point of a help topic.

Browse sequence

Sequentially linked topics for a specific subject in an online help. Users typically can use controls to change from one topic to the next.

Browsing

Scrolling

Moving the monitor display or content of a window horizontally or vertically.

Button

Sensitive interface element that starts a command.

CMS

Content Management System; a software application for creating and organizing text and multimedia contents in one source. The focus is on media-independent data management. CMS are often XML based and are supposed to be usable without programming or XML knowledge.

Command

Menu entry, menu point, menu option, menu function, instruction

Anything that generates an action in the user interface when clicked on. Commands can be accessed from menus, by clicking a button, or by using a keyboard shortcut.

Configuration

Settings

Long term settings for a product can be configured through commands. A configuration is in comparison to the adaptability of a technical nature and remains active until the configuration is changed.

Context free

General help

Help that is not directly connected to a specific user interface element in an application, for example an introduction or concept information.

Context menu

Popup menu, right-click menu

> A menu for a specific object that opens when the user clicks the right mouse button. A context menu shows only commands that are relevant for the current object.

Context sensitive

> Help that fits the current usage context, typically at dialog box or element level. Opposite of context free help. Compare also with sensitive.

Descender

> Extension of the letters g, p, q, y, or j below the base line.

Description

> Type of text that explains a specific circumstance. Compare to step-by-step instruction.

Dialog box

Dialog field, dialog, dialog window

> Interface element for interaction with the application. The dialog box is closed by clicking a button (such as OK or Cancel). Compare to window.

Dialog box help

Context sensitive help

> Context sensitive help at dialog box level. An explanation is displayed related to the current dialog box from which the help was called.

Direct help

F1 help

> Context sensitive help at element level. An explanation for the specific element is displayed for which the help was requested.

Drop-down text

> Text in a help that is only visible after the user clicked on a sensitive element. Drop-down text typically consists of one or more paragraphs. The topic content after the drop-down text is moved downward when the drop-down text is displayed. This is suitable for additional information for specific groups, such as novices. Compare to expandable text and popups.

Embedded help

Help that is part of the user interface of the application.

Expanded text

Text in an online help that is only displayed when the user clicks on a sensitive element. The text is shown in the same line right next to the sensitive element. The following text in the line moves accordingly. This is useful for explanations of abbreviations or technical terms. Compare to drop-down text and popups.

Eyecatcher

Visual attention, highlighter

Accentuation within the text, for example a different color or an (animated) graphic.

Favorite

User-specific entry point for help.

Graphical User Interface

GUI, user interface

Interface displayed on screen that allows for communication between persons and products, which are operated by the user through an application or a user assistance system.

Help agent

A program that brokers between user and online help and that accepts queries in natural language. The help agent replies to the query with various answers. The user can select the most suitable answer.

Help Authoring Tool

HAT

Application that is used for creating online help and documentation.

Help format

Target system

Specifies the format for the help, for example Winhelp or JavaHelp.

Help type

Part of user assistance, for example a tool tip or context sensitive help.

Help window

Help viewer

> Window that contains the online help and provides all necessary control elements.

Hierarchical navigation

> Structure, typically shown as tree view, that helps the user to find their way through a large amount of information, for example, the table of contents of an online help or the tree view in a file explorer.

Highlighted

Marked

> Text area that is marked by a different font or color. This can be used for options or search terms.

Hypertext

> Information provided as a network of pages that can be navigated by the user via mouse clicks. It is typically organized in a tree structure, but cross-references are possible. A hypertext consists of topics that contain information and links that explicitly create the logical connection between the topics. There is no defined sequence, every user has to find his or her own way. Hypertexts are characterized by non-linearity and individualization.

Icon

Symbol, button

> An icon is a pictograph with a special meaning. An icon can also be context-sensitive.

Image map

> Graphic that contains various links.

Information group

Information type

> Information that fulfills a specific function for the user, for example, prerequisites for operations instructions, a single instruction step, or a hint.

Information type

Information group

> Topics can be associated with different, self-defined information types, for example, target groups: beginner, advanced, expert. Information types are used to display topics based on the target audience.

Interaction

> Action of the user and reaction of the product through the user interface.

Legibility

> Metric for the reading speed of text. A text with a high legibility can be read faster than one with poor legibility. Legibility directly depends on the design of the characters, lines, and areas (typography) and is one criterion for the readability of a text.

Link

Hyperlink, jump, reference

> Sensitive element that acts as a reference for the target spot.

Markup

Typography, display instrument

> Main category of formal text markup for accentuation of important passages or defined elements. Markups are, for example, bold, cursive, underlined, or colored.

Master page

> Page template for a target that is applied during build.

Menu

Drop-down menu, sub-menu

> A collection of commands that are presented under a main category. Also: menu bar, main menu, sub-menu, context menu

Message

Info message, error message

> Output of the product reporting on status, or an error, with information on how to prevent the problem, shown in its own dialog box or in a status bar.

Navigation

Controls that allow the user to browse through a particular amount of data, for example, forward or backward. Compare to hierarchical navigation.

Normal element

Text or picture that is not context-sensitive.

Online help

Help system, help

Part of the secondary assistance: information for selective support while using a product.

Online page, or short: Page

Page, web page, screen, display

Page that is displayed on screen and where browsing is possible. Also: page layout, page margins, start page, page title.

Operations instructions

Step-by-step instructions, work instructions, directions, manual

Instructions describing each step of a task needed to complete the task successfully. Operations instructions are a specific type of text that should be marked up accordingly (1., 2., ...). Operations instructions contain, besides the individual steps, the goal description, the prerequisites, and the feedback from the application.

Overlayed information

Main category for information such as texts, tables, graphics, and so forth that is displayed only after the user clicked a sensitive element. The various display types are: expanding text, drop-down text, and popups.

Paragraph

Section, passage

Coherent lines of text that express one thought.

Popup

Text in a help that is only displayed when users click on a sensitive element. After the click, the text or image is displayed in a separate, but dependent window.

Primary assistance

> All information that is visible on first sight in the product on screen (for example, labeling in the user interface). Compare to user assistance, secondary user assistance.

Proprietary

> File formats or hardware that do not follow commonly accepted standards, such as self-made products or products that can only be run on specific platforms.

Proxy

> Program element that is executed during a build.

Readability

> Linguistic composition, also semantic (such as choice of word, sentence structure) of a text and a criterion for how easy a text can be read and understood.

Sans-serif font

> Fonts based on the Antiqua font, often with linear strokes that have no serifs.

Screen shot

Snapshot, capture

> Depiction of the entire monitor display, of an application window, or parts thereof.

Secondary assistance

> All the information that is not visible on first sight in the user interface, but that is only accessible after the user performed an activity (such as a tool top when moving the mouse pointer over an object). Compare to primary user assistance, user assistance.

Sensitive element

Hotspot

> Symbols or text that execute a function (help) or a command (application) when the user clicks on them, for example, a link to a different location. Compare to normal element, context sensitive, button.

Serif

> Small cross-bars at the up- and down strokes of characters.

Signal word

> Standardized term for example for warnings (such as "Caution", "Danger", "Warning") that should not be used outside of the designated context.

Skin

> Determines how a help windows looks like.

Spacing

> Increasing the distance between characters (as opposed to kerning where the distance between characters is reduced).

Tag

XML tag

> Markup for XML elements.

Text amount

> Quantitative amount of text.

Text type

Kind of text, text group

> Texts are differentiated based on their purpose: a description explains an issue, an instructive text is suitable for a manual. Compare to information type.

Tool tip

Bubble help

> Part of the secondary user assistance: short information for a user interface element that is displayed when hovering the mouse pointer over the object.

Topic

Subject, node

> Logical information unit of help.

Tracking

> Distance of characters from each other. When the distance is increased it is called spacing, when the distance is decreased it is called kerning. The tracking is changed for design purposes or to fit text into a given space.

Unicode

International standard character set for the international exchange of files and their editing. Unicode does not only cover the Latin character set, but represents characters with 16 bit so that a total of 65,536 characters can be coded. Characters that are used in multiple languages are coded only once in Unicode, which leads to a huge reduction in characters to be coded especially for Chinese, Japanese, and Korean characters.

Usability

User-friendliness, ease of use

How usable a product or service is.

Usability test

Examination of the usability of a software or hardware product by letting potential users work with it.

User

Operator

Person who works at a computer.

User Assistance

User assistance includes all types of information that supports the user in using the software product on screen. User assistance offers specific information or help for the product. A differentiation is made between primary assistance and secondary assistance.

User interface description

Reference, program description

Main term for the description of all elements in the user interface of a product.

User interface element

Control, button, control element

Any element of a user interface. User interface elements are also called control elements because the behavior of the product or the user assistance system is controlled through them. Examples are menus, buttons, windows, and labels.

Viewer system, short: Viewer

Display

Viewer application or display system, for example, the HTMLHelp Viewer.

Web

WWW

Graphically displayed portion of the Internet. Also: web browser, web application.

Window

Main window, secondary window, dialog box

Element of the user interface that can be equipped with a menu bar, tool bar, or navigation or workspace area. It is closed by a command or a button click.

Wizard

Assistant

Software feature that leads the user through a complex activity. A wizard can be started either by the user or by the application.

XML

eXtensible Markup Language; markup language for the display of hierarchically structured data using flat files (text files). XML is used predominantly for the data exchange between different IT systems, especially over the Internet.

Literature

Adkisson, Heidi (2002): Identifying De-Facto Standards for E-Commerce Web Sites, A thesis submitted in partial fulfillment of the requirements for the degree of Master of Science, University of Washington

Bartsch, Christian (2001): Die Verständlichkeit von Software-Hilfesystemen, Lübeck: Schmidt-Römhild

Ballstaedt, Steffen (1997): Wissensvermittlung. Die Gestaltung von Lernmaterial. Weinheim: Beltz Psychologische Verlags Union

Closs, Sissi (2007): Single Source Publishing – Topicorientierte Strukturierung und DITA, entwickler press

Conklin, J. (1987): A Survey of Hypertext, MCC Technical Report No. STP-356, Rev., Dezember 1987

Day, Don, **Priestley**, Michael, **Schell**, David (2005): Introduction to the Darwin Information Typing Architecture, http://www.ibm.com/developerworks/xml/library/x-dita1/.

Dentz, Dorothea (2001): Informationsdesign für technische Dokumentation in einem Dokumentenmanagementsystem. In: J. Hennig und M. Tjarks-Sobhani (Hrsg.): Informations- und Wissensmanagement für technische Dokumentation. Lübeck: Schmidt-Römhild

Dyson, Mary C, (2005): How do We Read Text on Screen, in Creation, Use and Deployment of Digital Information, Edited by H. van Oostendorp. L. Breure and A. Dillon, New Jersey: Erlbaum

Edelmann, Anja (2003): Hypertextbasierte Softwaredokumentation, Eine experimentelle Untersuchung zur Rezeption, Lübeck: Schmidt-Römhild

Grünwied, Gertrud (2005): Software-Dokumentation, Grundlagen – Praxis – Lösungen, Renningen: expert verlag

Horn, R. E. (2001): Knowledge Mapping for Complex Social Messes, http://www.stanford.edu/~rhorn

Klante, Palle (2007): Barrierefreie Informationsangebote – Accessability, In: J. Hennig und M. Tjarks-Sobhani (Hrsg.): Usability und technische Dokumentation. Lübeck: Schmidt-Römhild

Knopp, Sandra (2000): Aufbau, Gestaltung und Struktur von Online-Hilfesystemen. Im Kontext der Mensch-Computer-Interaktion, Lübeck: Schmidt-Römhild

Krömker, Heidi (2007): Usability – Stand der Forschung, In: J. Hennig und M. Tjarks-Sobhani (Hrsg.): Usability und technische Dokumentation. Lübeck: Schmidt-Römhild

Krug, Steve (2002): Don't make me think: Web-Usability – das intuitive Web, Übers. aus dem Amerik. von Jürgen Dubau, Bonn: Mitp-Verlag

Lehrndorfer, Anne (1999): Zielgruppengerechtes Schreiben, In: J. Hennig und M. Tjarks-Sobhani (Hrsg.): Verständlichkeit und Nutzungsfreundlichkeit von technischer Dokumentation. Lübeck: Schmidt-Römhild

Ley, Martin (2005): Kontrollierte Textstrukturen – Ein (linguistischens) Informationsmodell für die technische Kommunikation, Inaugural Dissertation, Justus Liebieg Ubiversität, Gießen

Mohs, C., **Naumann**, A. & **Kindsmüller**, M. (2007): Mensch-Technik-Interaktion: intuitiv, erwartungskonform oder vertraut? in MMI Interaktiv, Nr. 13

Muthig, J. und **Schäflein-Armbruster**, R. (2000): Funktionsdesign. Eine universelle und flexible Standardisierungstechnik. In: W. Kurz und B. Wallin-Felkner (Hrsg.): Praxishandbuch Technische Dokumentation. Loseblattwerk. Augsburg: WEKA

Nielsen, Jacob (2001): Designing Web Usability – Erfolg des Einfachen. 2. überarb. Auflage, München: Markt + Technik

Paivio, A. (1979): Imagery and verbal processes. Hillsdale, New Jersey: Erlbaum

Pernice K. & **Nielsen**, J. (2001): Beyond ALT Text, Making the Web Easy to Use for Users with Disabilities, Norman Nielsen Group, Fremont

Priestley, Michael (2005): Specializing topic types in DITA, http://www.ibm.com/developerworks/xml/library/x-dita2/

Spool, J., **Scanlon**, T., **Schroeder**, W., **Snyder**, C. & **DeAngelo**, T. (1999): Web Site Usability. A Designers Guide. San Francisco: Morgan Kaufman

Standford Encyclopedia of Philosophie, Center for the Study of Language and Information, Stanford University, Stanford, CA, http://plato.stanford.edu/

tekom e.V. (Hrsg) (2004): Kriterien zur Beurteilung von Online-Informationen, Stuttgart

Thissen, Frank (2001): Screen-Design-Handbuch: Effektiv informieren und kommunizieren mit Multimedia. 2. überarb. und erw. Aufl. Berlin: Springer

Wieser, Verena (2004): Usability versus Design – ein Widerspruch? Theorie und Praxis der Gestaltung von Websites, Studien der Erlanger Buchwissenschaft VI: Universität Erlangen

Codes and Standards

IEEE 1063 (2001): Standard for Software User Documentation

DIN EN ISO 6385 (2004-05): Grundsätze der Ergonomie für die Gestaltung von Arbeitssystemen (ISO 6385:2004); Deutsche Fassung EN ISO 6385:2004

DIN EN ISO 9241: Ergonomische Anforderungen für Bürotätigkeiten mit Bildschirmgeräten

Teil 110: Grundsätze der Dialoggestaltung (ersetzt den bisherigen Teil 10)

Teil 11: Anforderungen an die Gebrauchstauglichkeit

Teil 12: Informationsdarstellung

Teil 171: Leitlinien für die Zugänglichkeit von Software

DIN EN ISO 13407 (2000): Benutzer-orientierte Gestaltung interaktiver Systeme

DIN EN ISO 14915: SW-Ergonomie für Multimedia-Benutzerschnittstellen

Teil 1: Gestaltungsgrundsätze und Rahmenbedingungen

Teil 2: Multimedia – Navigation und Steuerung

Teil 3: Auswahl und Kombination von Medien

ISO/IEC 15910 (1999): Information technology – Software user documentation process

ISO/IEC 18019 (2004): Software and system engineering – Guidelines for the design and preparation of user documentation for application software

DIN 33455: Barrierefreie Produkte

DIN VDE 1000 Teil 10: Anforderungen an im Bereich der Elektrotechnik tätige Personen

tekom e.V. (2006): QualiAssistent, http://www.tekom.de/index_neu.jsp? url=/servlet/ControllerGUI?action=voll&id=1981

W3C (2004): Accessibility Guideline, http://www.w3.org/WAI/GL/WCAG20/

Index

8525366R0

Made in the USA
Lexington, KY
09 February 2011